Essays on

Gender Inequality

Migration Drivers

And

Realising Africa's Potentials

Edited by

Olivia Bola J-Olajide Aluko
LLB, B.L, MA (Law)

Reinvent African Diaspora Network

Essays on Gender Inequality, Migration Drivers, and Realising Africa's Potentials

Copyright © 2023 by Olivia Bola J-Olajide Aluko

Published by

Sophos Books

Croydon

CR0 0AZ

publishwithsophos@gmail.com

In collaboration with

Reinvent Africa Diaspora Network (RADET) Ltd.

https://www.reinvent3r.org

admin@reinvent3r.org

ISBN 978-1-905669-80-6

Advanced editing and proof reading by University Proofreading Services, Chalfont, Pennsylvania, USA.

Printed in the United Kingdom

CONTENTS

Contributors   6

Biography   7

Preface   9

PART 1: GENDER INEQUALITY

1   **Sociological and Economic perspectives of Gender Inequality**

Olivia Bola J-Olajide Aluko, LLB, B.L, MA (Law)   18

2   **Gender Inequality and Career aspirations**

Sophia Aluko   57

3   **A Case for Re-enacting Gender Based Violence (GBV)**

Ola-Kris Akinola, PhD.   67

4   **The Impact of Gender-based Violence on Mental Health**

Lade Olugbemi, BA, LLB, LLM   73

5   **Domestic Abuse in Africa – A Focus on Nigeria**

Margaret O. Ojo   87

PART 2: MIGRATION DRIVERS

6 Trends in African Migration

Olivia Bola J-Olajide Aluko, LLB, B.L, MA (Law)   114

7 African Migration and Significance: Perspective of Kenya Health Sector

Martha Nyawira Chege   168

8 An Overview of Return Migration to Ghana

Olivia Bola J-Olajide Aluko, LLB. B.L MA (Law)   176

9 The Challenges of African Identity in the UK

Joseph Adamson   189

PART 3: REALISING AFRICA'S POTENTIALS

10 From Brain Drain to Brain Gain

Adeoye Ademola   196

11 Social Responsibility: The New Normal for Solidarity

Mar Introini, PhD   200

12 Untapped Opportunities in Africa

Olajide Abiola   204

13 The Impact of Digital Transformation on Economic Growth

Akintola Akinsanya 210

14 Youth Identity and the Challenges

Olivia Bola J-Olajide Aluko, LLB. B.L MA (Law) 220

15 Africa's Youth Trailblazer in Commerce and Innovation (A focus on Nigeria)

Adetunji Omotola BSc, MA, LLB, B.L 243

16 Adapting Education to Learners' Needs

Christian Nonso 251

CONTRIBUTORS

Abiola, Olajide

Adamson, Joseph

Adeoye, Ademola

Akinola, Ola-Kris PhD

Akinsanya, Akintola

Aluko, Sophia

Chege, Martha Nyawira

Introini, Mar PhD

J-Olajide Aluko, Olivia Bola LLB, B.L, MA (Law)

Nonso, Christian

Ojo, O. Margaret

Olugbemi, Lade Hephzibah BA, LLB, LLM

Omotola, Adetunji BSc, MA, LLB, B.L

BIOGRAPHY

Olivia Bola J-Olajide Aluko

Olivia Bola J-Olajide Aluko LLB, B.L, MA (Law) is a lawyer, sustainable development advocate, migration scholar, facilitator, journal author, and international speaker. She began her career in Nigeria, West Africa and progressed to complete her master's degree in Migration and Law at the world class research institution Queen Mary's University of London.

Olivia is an inspirational writer and community advocate widely known for her work on community cohesion and peaceful co-existence with migrants. She is an alumna of the Refugees as Rebuilders training programme based in the UK.

Olivia is a respected community leader who strives to advance others' rights ranging from justice to gender equality. She has spoken on many platforms at the local, national and international levels to enhance women's safety and security and engage in debates about migration and diaspora in both academic and non-academic circles. Olivia has a strong proclivity for the Human Security Pillars, and she uses her well-researched analysis to debunk negative migration stories.

Olivia is a regular speaker at the largest global scholarly conference on migration. She is also a member of various networks, including the World Association for Sustainable Development (WASD), the

Association for the Study of Ethnicity and Nationalism (ASEN) and Initiatives of Change UK (IOFC). In addition, Olivia is the CEO of REOPASS Family Navigators, Ltd, a non-profit organisation that exists to work with and signpost families that have been separated and/or divorced. She is also the chairperson of Reinvent African Diaspora Network, UK (RADET) an educational initiative that stimulates debate on migration and diaspora studies through roundtable discussions, conferences and training in furtherance of 'Reinventing Africa' based on the principles elaborated in the UN Sustainable Development Goals.

Olivia is a mental aid first aider and a member of the Board of the Nous organisation UK, a mental health awareness outfit. As vice president of the Africa Security Forum, she has diligently worked to improve community understanding of domestic violence issues and women-related security challenges. Olivia has published three books, including the non-fiction volumes *Africans in the UK: Migration, Integration and Significance*; *Globalisation, Human Security and Social Inclusion*, and the novel *Life in the Abrodi*. She is currently working on her next book series.

PREFACE

Olivia Bola J-Olajide Aluko

This series of essays was compiled against the backdrop of social and economic challenges impacting the world, with a special focus on the Sub-Saharan African countries.

Gender inequality, also referred to as 'gender discrimination', is a widespread social problem. This term is defined as the unfair treatment of individuals based on one 's gender. Gender-based inequality is a practice that limits girls and women from accessing education, career opportunities, political advancement, and in some places where women are paid less salary because of their gender, access to certain jobs. Gender inequality is also a root cause of violence against women and girls. Whilst the women may be granted more social and political rights in some places than others, there is no country where gender equality has been achieved. From everyday sexism to brutally enforced regimes of gender differentiation, biological difference continues to bring with it varying—and often radically distinct—implications (Bates, 2016).

These discriminatory practices not only hamper the achievement of gender equality, but also negatively impact economic growth. Gender-based discrimination in social institutions costs the global economy up to USD 12 trillion (Ferrant & Kolev, 2016). A United Nations Women (UN Women) report released in 2016 estimated the global cost of violence against women to be USD 1.5 trillion, equivalent to approximately 2% of the global gross domestic product (GDP), or roughly the size of the entire Canadian economy (UN Women, 2016).

Addressing this reality and the part that it continues to play in our various communities is the subject of this book. The manifold factors contributing to gender-based inequality in Africa include ascribing women a lower status in society and normalising acts of violence towards women, which is a habit that runs deep in many countries. Moreover, there are still social norms that support the use of violence as a means of conflict resolution in many African states.

A 2016 report by the UN Development Programme (2016) reported that persistent gender inequality has severely limited sub-Saharan Africa's potential, with an estimated yearly loss of USD 95 billion. At the current rate, it could take Africa more than 140 years to achieve gender parity. Some of the most egregious issues inhibiting women's equality include religious and cultural practices such as rigid traditions, a lack of medical care, poverty, and a lack of empowerment (McKinsey Global Institute, 2019). Gender inequality can be a powerful factor leading to migration when women have economic, political and social expectations that cannot be realised in their country of origin.

African migration is being driven by a varied combination of push-pull factors impacting each country. The primary push factors are conflict, repressive governance, and limited economic opportunities. However, as McAuliffe and Koser (2017, p. 1) describe, 'Orderly movement has largely been the norm, and this has contributed to growth in economies, increased human development, the capacity to protect large numbers of people facing persecution, and the ability of hundreds of millions of people to forge meaningful lives abroad. Concomitantly, there is a perception that other countries and regions, particularly some non-industrialised nations and peoples, have perhaps not fared as well, and the benefits of international migration could perhaps be described as uneven. Against this backdrop, there is growing concern that the less desirable aspects of international migration are increasing in significance and magnitude: the growth in irregular migration (including people smuggling and human trafficking); the increasing restrictiveness of migration-receiving countries' entry policies; a sense that national identities are being threatened (not just that they are changing); rising exploitation of migrants all the way along the migration pathway; and increasing harm to migrants, including substantial numbers of deaths during journeys (Brian & Laczko, 2014), all threaten the overall dividends of international migration.'

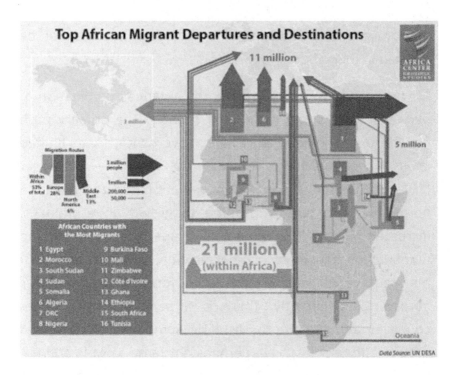

Source: <u>African Migration Trends to Watch in 2022 – Africa Center for Strategic Studies</u>

The term 'African Potentials' refers to the knowledge, systems, practices, ideas and values created and implemented in African societies that are expected to contribute to overcoming various challenges and promoting people's wellbeing. There is an enormous untapped wealth of resources in Africa, and many countries have the opportunity to turn that potential wealth into gains for people living across the income spectrum. Africa's potential is about empowering Africans so that they do not have to leave the country to migrate.

For instance, Youth between ages 15 and 24 constitute 20 percent of sub-Saharan Africa's total population (Cornell Research, 2022) Notably, many of these youth are not in education, employment, or training. However, digital technologies are driving change across sub-Saharan Africa. As Eugene Kiminine, an ICT expert in Kigali, explains, 'Digital consumers across sub-Saharan Africa are fueling customer growth and driving the adoption of new mobile services needed to empower lives and transform businesses on the continent' (Kiminine, quoted by Tasamba, 2019). From Nigeria, Kenya, Tunisia to Egypt, and Libya, among others, African youths have demonstrated their ability to use technology to drive social and political changes in their environment.

REFERENCES

Africa Center for Strategic Studies (2021, 21 December). African migration trends to watch in 2022. https://africacenter.org/spotlight/african-migration-trends-to-watch-in-2022/

Bates, L. (2016). *Everyday sexism: The project that inspired a worldwide movement*. New York: St. Martin's Publishing Group.

Brian, T., & Laczko. F. (Eds.) (2014). *Fatal journeys : tracking lives lost during migration*. Geneva: International Organization for Migration.

Cornell Research (2022). *The exploding youth population in sub-Saharan Africa*. https://research.cornell.edu/research/exploding-youth-population-sub-saharan-africa

Ferrant, G. & Kolev, A. (2016). *The economic cost of gender-based discrimination in social institutions.* OECD Development Centre. https://www.oecd.org/dev/development-gender/SIGI_cost_final.pdf

McAuliffe, M. & Koser, K. (2016). *A long way to go: Irregular migration patterns, processes, drivers and decision-making.* ANU Press.

McKinsey Global Institute (2019, 24 November). *The power of parity: Advancing women's equality in Africa*. https://www.mckinsey.com/featured-insights/gender-equality/the-power-of-parity-advancing-womens-equality-in-africa

Tasamba, J. (2019, 14 August). *Sub-Saharan Africa's future linked to technology: Digitalization has impacted everything in region, from communications to agriculture, says ICT expert*. Analadu Agency. https://www.aa.com.tr/en/africa/sub-saharan-africa-s-future-linked-to-technology/1556198

UN Development Programme (2016, 28 August). *Africa human development report 2016*. https://www.undp.org/publications/africa-human-development-report-2016

UN Women (2016, 21 September). *The economic costs of violence against women*. Remarks by UN Assistant Secretary General and Deputy Executive Director of UN Women, Lakshmi Puri at the high-level discussion on the 'Economic cost of violence against women'. https://www.unwomen.org/en/news/stories/2016/9/speech-by-lakshmi-puri-on-economic-costs-of-violence-against-women

PART 1

Essays on

Gender Inequality

1

SOCIOLOGICAL AND ECONOMIC
PERSPECTIVES OF GENDER INEQUALITY

Olivia B J-Olajide Aluko

Gender inequality remains pervasive around the globe, as reflected in disparities in household authority and bargaining power, access to education and forms of employment, occupation, earnings, political representation, and leadership. These gaps are particularly glaring in May parts of the developing world, where according to UNESCO Institute for Statistics (UIS, 2016) estimates, 15 million girls of primary-school age—more than half of them in sub-Saharan Africa—will never enter a classroom and 130 million girls between the age of 6 and 17 will never complete primary or secondary education. Although gaps in employment and pay are closing in developing countries, the prevalence of gender inequality remains significant, particularly in South Asia, the Middle East and North Africa (Klasen and Lamanna 2009). Women continue to be severely underrepresented among top positions— representing less than 30% of managers even in the most developed countries (World Bank 2001), and women are generally employed in a limited number of sectors; fewer women have access to white collar jobs and large proportions are confined to garment production, manufacturing and domestic work. In many countries, women also have reduced access to entrepreneurship opportunities compared with men.

In addition to undermining the goal to achieve universal human rights, economic models have demonstrated that gender gaps in the labour market result in negative impacts on economic development reducing per capita income as well as productivity (Cuberes and Teigner 2012; Teigner and Cuberes 2014). Building the necessary manpower to actualise economic development cannot be achieved without the empowerment of women (Cook 1994). To achieve economic development, it is critical to enhance the engagement of the female population not only in economic activities but also in political representation and governance.

Although there have been some improvements in gender equality in terms of political participation and wages, progress has lagged because we live in a world where children are socialised to accept male dominance and female subservience (York 2011). Girls and women are particularly demeaned in many developing countries, where they have little or no rights; consequently, they are subject to all manner of forms of exploitation, ranging from intimate partner violence to sexual violence.

The action points of the Sustainable Development Goals (SDG) highlight the centrality of gender equality. It seems impossible to achieve significant success in any of the SDG spheres, including ensuring quality health care and education or reducing poverty, ending hunger, or creating opportunities for sustainable employment, without achieving reducing gender inequalities. In the context of sub-Saharan Africa, it is imperative to empower women in order for economic growth and social sustainability to reach its full potential (Coquery 2018).

This study examines the links between gender inequality, gender-based violence, economic development and migration in the context of sub-Saharan Africa. We also consider the vulnerability of women during migration, and briefly highlight the impacts of the 2020 COVID-19 pandemic on African women before presenting ideas regarding ways that individuals, organisations, and governments can work together towards gender equality.

AN OVERVIEW OF GENDER INEQUALITY

Gender inequality is the systemic hierarchy between men and women in terms of material resources, power and status (Ridgeway 2011, p.4). Gender inequality arises from differences in biology through chromosomes, brain structure, and hormonal differences, which are then reflected in socially constructed gender roles. For millennia, men in many of the world's societies have been taught that they were superior to women and deserved special privileges, such as power over family decision-making, legal ownership over women and their property, and political leadership and governance.

In many societies, women's livelihoods were historically dependent on who they married, as their roles were traditionally viewed as being limited to child-rearing and managing the home, whereas the husband was the breadwinner who acted as the head of the household and primary decision-maker. Prior to marriage, daughters were under their fathers' control, and upon becoming married, wives fell under the protection of their husbands. Married couples often became one person in the eyes of the law, and under coverture, women could not sign legal documents, enter into contracts, obtain education, or retain a salary or own property against her husband's wishes (Beattie and Stevens 2013). Even in cases when women had wealth in their own right prior to marriage, this became the property of their husbands. Women also faced restricted inheritance rights, which were typically limited to personal effects rather than land or property, and in societies where male primogeniture prevailed, female heirs could only benefit in the absence of a male sibling (Beattie and Stevens 2013). Women were refused the right to vote, and in the education domain, girls in western countries generally only received primary and secondary level schooling, and most universities were open only to men.

It has only been over the past two centuries that women have begun to gain traction in the struggle for equal rights, and these victories have been uneven and hard won. With the rise of women's rights organisations in the mid-19th century, the US Married Women's Property Acts extended property rights to women between 1839 and 1895 (Custer 2013), and similar laws were passed in Sweden in the 1870s and 1880s; however, in the US and most European countries the coverture system legally remained in force well into the 20th century (Canaday 2008). Married French women were not granted the right to work without their husband's consent until 1965 (Perry 2002), and husband's paternal authority over the family was not abolished until 1970 (Ferrand 2008). The US Supreme Court did not declare male rule in marriage to be constitutional until 1980, and Switzerland did not establish gender equality in marriage until 1988 (Wecker 2016). Although Sweden had established universal suffrage in the 18th century and Australia and New Zealand granted women the right to vote in the late 19th century, most western countries did not legalise women's suffrage until 1918-1920, and women could not vote in France until 1944, in Greece until 1952, and Switzerland until 1971 (Ramirez et al. 1997).

Although there have been vital improvements in women's rights in developed countries, gender inequality continues to be a major barrier to human development in countries of the Global South, including Latin America, parts of Asia, and Africa. According to UNCSW (1994), although women are over half of the world's population, they perform two-thirds of the world's work while receiving only one-tenth of the world's income and owning one-hundredth of the world's property. Even in most of the western world, women are still paid less than men for performing the same jobs, and very few organisations can boast of having women on their board of directors. Those women who are able to ascend the career ladder have often been forced to sacrifice their family lives. In recent years, activists campaigning against gender inequality have highlighted the loss to countries when women are not allowed to participate economically, socially and politically. The annual report by the United Nations Development Programme (UNDP, 2010), which was later incorporated as the Gender Inequality Index (GID) emphasised that the discrimination and underrepresentation of women in health, education, politics, work and other parts of life has repercussions for the development of their capabilities and their freedom of choice.

GENDER INEQUALITY IN SUB-SAHARAN AFRICA

Africa is a continent with different cultures and diverse beliefs. For example, in some parts of West Africa, women can wear trousers and are not required to cover their heads; however, in others, socio-cultural norms enforce adherence to strict codes requiring more 'modest dress'. The same also applies to women's aspiration to be entrepreneurs, become professionals, and become involved in politics. Male and female roles vary in different regions; although forms of legal pluralism traditionally prevailed in matrilineal societies such as that of the Akan in Ghana, women have generally been subordinate to men in public and family life. For generations, however, gender roles and sexual attitudes have been changing, particularly in cities and other areas more open to western influence.

Gender inequality is not new in African societies and the fight to establish equal rights for women in social, economic and politics is an ongoing exercise. No appreciable development can be made at the local, national or international scales without recognizing girls and women as equal players and empowering, up-skilling and investing in them.   African societies have long perceived African woman as being subservient to men and unable to thrive without the support of their husbands. In traditional African societies, it was taught that girls are inferior to boys; the latter must always be respected and their needs must take priority over those of girls.   Many African societies are organised patrilineally, and thus are dependent on male heirs to continue the lineage and secure the family's prosperity. Thus, many African societies have traditionally favoured sons over daughters; even today, stories abound of men who have ousted their spouses from the home for their failure to bear male children or taken additional wives, ignoring the fact that conceptualisation results from the combination of chromosomes from both men and women. In many villages, people tend to have larger families, as women are forced to continue conceiving until a male child is produced. Because girls are expected to eventually leave the family home to marry, much less emphasis is given to their education and wellbeing.

African traditional culture stresses that men and women have different roles in society, and girls and boys are socialised to adhere to those norms. For example, girls are usually responsible for tasks such assisting their mothers with cooking and gathering firewood and water, whereas boys help hunt and fish. These roles persist into adulthood, when women become responsible for the children and home and in many cases become subordinated to their husbands. Compared with 0% of developed nations, 22% percent of sub-Saharan countries have not passed laws granting women equal property rights in marriage, 30% have not established equal inheritance for sons and daughters, and 24% do not acknowledge a woman's right to inherit from her spouse (United Nations Women [UNW], 2016).

Although there have been improvements in combatting gender inequality with regards to education and employment in many African societies, a great deal still needs to be done to ensure that women's efforts and contributions to both the economic and social strata of their nations are not taken for granted. Sub-Saharan Africa is among the world's lowest performers in gender equality measures such as education, wages, and labour market and political participation. Of the bottom 20 countries on the Equal Measures 2030 (EM2030 2019), Sustainable Development Goals (SDG) Index, 17 are in Sub-Saharan Africa, and among the ten lowest rankings on this measure, nine are sub-Saharan African countries—Sierra Leone, Liberia, Nigeria, Mali, Mauritania, Niger, Congo, DR Congo, and Chad.

Educational inequality

Many families still choose to send only male children to school, as they believe that there is no benefit to educating girls, who will not contribute to the family's wealth after marriage. Girls comprise nearly 19 million of the 34.2 million primary aged children who are out of school in sub-Saharan Africa, including 5.5 million in Nigeria, particularly in the northern regions, as well as over one million in Ethiopia (UIS 2016). Overall, the gender gap in education remains over 20% in Togo (22.2%); Angola (24.1%); Mali (24.3%); Benin (26.7%), and reaches 35-40% in Guinea (32%); Democratic Republic of the Congo (34.2%), and Chad (41.1%; World Economic Forum, 2019).

The consequences of educational inequality are vast. Girls who are unable to complete their education often become dependent on male relatives or husbands and are forced to turn to them for financial support. Many undereducated girls are forced to provide unpaid labour at home or marry younger, which consequences for their independence, health and well-being. Women who only complete primary or secondary school also face restrictions in the labour market, where they often occupy low wage jobs as domestic workers or in manufacturing, and a disproportionate number end up working in insecure jobs in the informal economy.

Wages and labour force participation

Although the gap in women's labour force participation in sub-Saharan Africa is the lowest of all regions at 13% (UNW 2016), there are wide variations across countries, and the gap rises as high as 53.5% in Cote d'Ivoire and 64% in Senegal (World Economic Forum 2019). On average, women with children in sub-Saharan Africa earn 34% less than men for equal work; that figure rises to over 50% in Ethiopia and Lesotho, and over 65% in Ghana and Lesotho (World Economic Forum 2019). Estimates indicate that between 75% and 89% of African women are restricted to working in the informal economy, leaving them unprotected in cases of theft, sexual harassment and discrimination (International Labour Organization 2018; UNW 2016). Although women occupy 49% of senior positions in Cameroon, in other parts of the region the proportion ranges from 14–30% (World Economic Forum 2019).

In many African cultures, even if a woman is progressing economically, she may be forced to lie to the extended family and the people in the community that it was her husband who is economically empowered. Restricting women from entrepreneurship and the labour force has consequences for economic growth. Economic modelling has demonstrated that excluding women from entrepreneurship reduced the average output per worker by nearly 12% and barring them from the labour force would reduce per capita income by almost 40% (Cuberes and Teigner 2012; Teigner and Cuberes 2014). A growth decomposition analysis released by the International Monetary Fund (IMF) revealed that average annual GDP per capita growth in sub-Saharan African countries could be increased by up to 0.9% if income and gender inequality were reduced even to the levels observed in the Association of South East Asian Nations (ASEAN; Hakura et al. 2016). A McKinsey Global Institute report indicated that Nigeria's gross domestic product (GDP) could grow by 23% ($229 billion) by 2025 if women participated in the economy to the same extent as men (Woetzel et 1l. 2015).

Political participation

Research indicates that higher proportions of female lawmakers are often reflected in lower corruption, increased citizen confidence in democratic institutions and government accountability, and more legislation promoting the wellbeing of women and children (Vogelstein 2016).

Women's participation in the political sphere remains relatively low in sub-Saharan Africa. Rwanda (which also has significantly lower wage and education gaps), South Africa and Ethiopia are among the world's top performers with up to 50% of women in parliament and more than 48% of women in ministerial positions, Rwanda (61%), Namibia (46%), South Africa (42%), and Senegal (42%) all ranked among the world's top ten countries in the 2019 SDG Gender Index in terms of women in parliament (EM2030 2019). When examining the percentage of women in parliament and ministry combined, Rwanda and South Africa retain high global ranking with 47% and 42% of women in government, respectively, while Uganda and Zambia have also reached a certain level of parity with 37% and 33% of women in government, respectively (EM 2030 2019). Ethiopia has recently made notable progress in this regard, as Prime Minister Abiy Ahmed reshuffled the cabinet to appoint women to half of all cabinet posts, and parliament appointed its first female president. In contrast, women occupy only 20–30% and 8–18% of parliament seats and ministerial positions in most other parts of the region. Nigeria is the sub-Saharan Africa's worst performer in terms of parliamentary representation, only 3.4% of which are occupied by women (World Economic Forum 2019).

CASE STUDY OF AFRICAN GENDER INEQUALITY: NIGERIA

Nigeria's population of over 196 million is the highest in Africa and is ranked seventh in the world (UNDP 2005). However, Nigeria ranks 118 of 134 countries in the Gender Equality Index (GEI) (Randriamaro 2012). Thirty-eight percent of women in Nigeria lack formal education compared with 25% of men, and only 4% of women have obtained higher education versus 7% of their male counterparts.

According to the World Poverty Clock, the number of Nigerians who are extremely poor and living on under $1.90 a day is now 94 million and rising (World Data Lab 2020). However, the true scale of the poverty problem in Nigeria becomes clearer when one considers that women, who make up slightly less than 50% of Nigeria's population, account for more than 70% of those in extreme poverty.

Hence, as in many other parts of the developing world, poverty in Nigeria is a gender issue, as are other massive inequalities across other socio-political determinants (Obiukwu 2019). Females in Nigeria are short-changed in every sector. According to the UNESCO Institute for Statistics (2020), up to 40% of girls are out of school, and those who do have access to education only remain in school for an average of nine years compared with 17 years in the developed world. Women's literacy rate of 59% lags significantly behind the 71% rate among men (Adejugbe and Adejugbe 2018). Nigerian women also experience one of the highest maternal mortality rates in the world, with over 800 maternal deaths per 100 000 live births for a total of approximately 58, 000 maternal deaths in 2015 compared with only 1,700 deaths in the world's 46 most developed countries (WHO 2019). In the political sphere, Nigeria ranks 181st out of 193 countries in parliamentary representation, comprising only 5.5% of Nigeria's elected officials and a little more than 16% of the federal ministers (Centre for Democracy and Development 2018).

In terms of finance, although 40% of Nigerian women are entrepreneurs, nearly 7 in 10 women are unbanked, and the aforementioned educational inequalities have resulted in a situation whereby a higher proportion of women than men are engaged in less lucrative, non-innovative entrepreneurial ventures (Olarewaju 2019). Although women made up 21.2 % of the labour force between the ages of 15 and 64 years compared to only 16.5% of men in 2015, women remain most heavily represented in the informal economy, and the number of men employed full time was over twice that of women (Adejugbe and Adejugbe 2018; National Bureau of Statistics 2017). Only a sparse proportion hold professional technical, administrative, or managerial positions. When women do achieve economic success, they are often forced to attribute their assets to their husbands in order to obscure their empowerment and avoid negative social repercussions.

GENDERED VIOLENCE IN SUB-SAHARAN AFRICA

According to the United Nations, violence against women is "Any act of gender-based violence that results in, or is likely to result in physical, sexual or mental harm or suffering to women, including threats of such acts, coercion or arbitrary deprivation of liberty, whether occurring in public or in private life" (General Assembly Resolution 48/104 Declaration on the Elimination of Violence against Women, 1993). Such violence takes many forms, including physical, emotional, psychological violence, forced marriage, financial and sexual abuse and exploitation, and gender-based homicide (femicide).

As in other parts of the world, gender-based violence (GBV) in sub-Saharan Africa is a by-product of traditional patriarchy and deeply entrenched socio-cultural norms that exalt the rights of boys and men over women. Often, there are no strict legal measures enacted or enforced to prohibit gender-based violence, and even in cases when governments have enacted laws prohibiting such behaviours, these norms are upheld by local community and religious leaders, and those who seek to contravene them risk social exclusion or even ostracism.

Indicators of gender-based violence can include how safe women feel at home, school, on the street or elsewhere in their communities. For example, EM2030 (2019) gender index includes measures of women's perceived safety walking alone at night. Whereas Rwanda (which performs high on most gender equality indices) ranks fifth on this global indicator, South Africa, a leader in women's political participation, ranks among the bottom three nations (EM2030 2019). A study by UNW reported that up to 20% of women in Nairobi schools have been sexually harassed, and a 2009 study found that 60% of schoolgirls in 10 Kenyan districts had experienced sexual harassment and 20% had been raped at school (Ruto 2009). A report by UNICEF Uganda (2013) revealed that 77.7% of primary school children and 82% of secondary school students in Uganda—the majority of whom were female—

had experienced sexual abuse from teachers and other staff, including 24% who were spoken to using sexual language, 18% who received marriage proposals and 25% who were touched in a sexual manner and 29% who were forced to watch pornography. A meta-analysis found that the proportion of female secondary and university students who reported having experienced GBV in an educational setting was 64% in Uganda, 51% in Ethiopia, and 45% in Nigeria (Beyene et al 2018). A study by the Uganda Bureau of Statistics (UBOS and ICF 2018) found that 19.1% of women who reported having been physically abused since the age of 15 identified a teacher as the perpetrator.

However, gender-based violence is primarily a family affair in many parts of Africa. For example, in Kenya, where between 39% and 47% of women aged between 15 and 49 years have experienced either physical or sexual violence and 33% have experienced sexual assault before the age of 18, strangers account for only 6% of GBV (Kenya Demographic and Health Survey [KDHS] 2015; UNICEF 2012; UNW 2016a). Similarly, in Nigeria, where 17.4% of women report having experienced physical or sexual violence, only 1.5% is attributed to non-partners [National Population Commission (NPC)] and ICF International, 2014). In such an environment, it is no surprise that many women are reluctant or afraid to report their abusers or otherwise act against them.

Intimate partner violence

Among the most prevalent forms of gender-based physical violence, intimate partner violence remains so deeply entrenched within the social fabric of many African societies that many women and men consider it to be a normal way of life. It is not uncommon to see women who are continuously abused but still justify or defend their abusive spouses' behaviour. For example, **'wife beating'** is regarded as a sign of love in certain Nigerian cultures, and women have been historically socialised to accept and sometimes encourage it. A 2016-17 Multiple Indicator Cluster Survey (MICS) reported that compared with only 21.5% of men, 33.7 of Nigerian women believed that husbands were justified in beating their wives for reasons ranging from burning the meal to leaving the house without informing him (National Bureau of Statistics [NBS] and UNICEF 2017). In Uganda, it is similarly believed that it is the right of a man to discipline his wife by beating her; in fact, it is a show of love and mercy that demonstrates the man's willingness to 'correct' her behaviour rather than divorcing her. Similarly, in many parts of Africa, people do not accept the concept of marital rape, as married women are perceived to have no right to sexual determination. Whereas globally, the prevalence of intimate partner violence is approximately 20%, these rates are higher in many African countries. Thus, the proportion of women reporting experiencing physical or sexual intimate partner violence in their lifetime was 51% in Democratic Republic of

Congo (Ministère du Plan et Suivi de la Mise en œuvre de la Révolution de la Modernité [MPSMRM] Congo et al. 2016), 50% in Uganda (UBOS and ICF 2018), 41% in Kenya (KDHS 2015), 28% in Ethiopia (Central Statistical Agency [CSA] 2016), and 21.3% in South Africa (UNW 2016a).

Intimate partner violence can also take on the form of financial abuse, which occurs when men limit women's economic empowerment by preventing them from engaging in paid work, constraining the number of hours or the type of work, or taking control of women's earnings.

There are many reasons why women in sub-Saharan Africa might feel compelled to remain with their abusers. Particularly in rural or conservative societies, divorce or single motherhood is a source of personal and family shame. When women approach family members or community or religious leaders regarding their abuse, they are often blamed for triggering their husbands' violence and advised to stay, fight for the marriage, adjust their own behaviour, and/or pray for the husband to become less violent. In some societies, a woman who leaves her abuser may face difficulties with child custody, be consigned to a life of poverty due to undeveloped alimony and palimony laws, and/or be condemned to a life of social isolation due to a lack of family or community support.

Female genital cutting

Although FGM/C, often referred to as female circumcision, is widely recognised as a violation of girls' human rights and a threat to their health, it remains prevalent in many parts of Africa. For example, Nigeria has the worlds' highest absolute number of girls who undergo female genital cutting, accounting for nearly 25% of the estimated 200 million women who have experienced such procedures. Nationally, 42% of Nigerian women have experienced female genital cutting (NBS and UNICEF 2017), including 62% of girls in the Yoruba ethnic group, 48% among the Igbo, and 39% of Hausa girls (Okeke et al. 2012; World Health Organization 2018). However, the national prevalence of FGM/C is over 90% in Sierra Leone Guinea, Djibouti and Somalia and near 90% in Sudan, Mali and Eritrea (UNICEF 2016).

Child marriage

Child marriage accounts for another widely practised form of gender-based violence in Africa. Child marriage is a form of forced marriage whereby girls who have not reached the legal age of consent are made to marry husbands chosen for them by their families. Child brides are generally less educated and tend to come from rural areas, and they are less likely to receive medical care during pregnancy than women who married over the age of 18, Moreover, under-five mortality and growth stunting are more common among children born of mothers under the age of 18 (Wodon et al. 2017). West and Central Africa (46%) and Eastern and Southern Africa (38%) have the second and third highest rates of child marriage for girls under 18, including 17% and 12% of girls under age 15, respectively (UNICEF 2014). Child marriage rates for girls under 18 are particularly prevalent in South Sudan (52%; Ministry of Health and National Bureau of Statistics, 2010), Sudan (50%; Central Bureau of Statistics (CBS) and UNICEF Sudan 2016), Democratic Republic of Congo (37%; MPSMRM et al. 2014). At 30% each, Niger and Chad each have the world's second highest rates of marriage for girls under age 15, closely followed by Ethiopia and Guinea, where the prevalence is approximately 27% in both cases (UNICEF 2014).

MIGRATION AS AN ALTERNATIVE TO GENDER INEQUALITY

Due to the above-described disparities, some women who are able to do so choose to migrate to other countries where their human rights can be protected and they can fulfil their educational and career potential. Others are forced to undertake the migration journey in order to flee conflict zones, poverty, or the negative impacts of natural disasters. Gender-related discrimination and violence, including forced marriage, domestic violence, female genital cutting prompt many girls and women to migrate in search of greater liberties and expanded social and economic opportunities. However, women are also particularly vulnerable to gender-based violence during the migration process, and are disproportionately affected by migrant trafficking. They are also significantly at risk of being recruited for forced labour in the sex trade or as domestic workers or caregivers.

The process of migration is experienced differently by women and men due to the impact of discrimination on women's journey. As the UNHCR Executive Committee (2006) reported, "women and girls can be exposed to particular protection problems related to their gender, their cultural and socio-economic position, and their legal status, which means they may be less likely than men and boys to be able to exercise their rights and therefore that specific action in favour of women and girls may be necessary to ensure they can enjoy protection and assistance on an equal basis with men and boys".

In the context of migration, the multiple forms of degradation that women endure due to the juxtaposition of their gender and their status of migrants and refugees place them in a specific situation of vulnerability. The migration process exacerbates gender discrimination and gender-based violence before, during and after their journey. As a result, women and girls are highly susceptible to trafficking as well as physical and sexual violence perpetrated by other migrants, smugglers, and law enforcement officers, among others. Migrant women are also more frequently affected by socioeconomic challenges in their destination countries, including unemployment, underemployment and insecure employment.

Nonetheless, there are many ways in which migration can promote greater empowerment of women. Migration to developed countries often expands girls' and women's access to education and professional qualifications, and migrant women can also earn better incomes and thereby attain higher degrees of autonomy and exercise new leadership roles. If these migrants return to their societies of origin, they can spread different behavioural norms and practices that improve the position of women. Many educated African women in Europe have established NGOs or conducted other work aimed to help promote gender equality and enhance the capacity of women to achieve economic independence and participate in decision-making in their societies of origin as well as abroad. For example, <u>ABANTU for Development (2020)</u> is a registered NGO established in 1991 by African women based in Europe that liaises with the Economic and Social Council (ECOSOC) of the United Nations to build networks in the fight against women's poverty in Europe as well as Africa and maintains offices in the UK, Kenya, Tanzania, Ghana and Nigeria. The co-founders of the African Women's Development Fund, a pan-African foundation that supports the work of women's rights organisations in Africa include Joanna Foster, a Ghanaian-born woman who obtained higher education in the UK, as well as Bisi Adeleye-Fayemi, a Liverpool-born woman who was educated in Nigeria and the UK and had previously served as the director of a London-based international development organisation for African women, and Hilda M. Tadria, a Uganda-born women's rights activist who obtained her master's and PhD in England and the United States, respectively (African Women's Development Fund 2020).

GENDER INEQUALITY IN THE COVID-19 ERA

COVID-19 pandemic is projected to infect at least 110 million people in sub-Saharan Africa and trigger severe economic consequences, including the first regional recession in nearly a quarter-century and an estimated 23 million more people being pushed into extreme poverty (Copley et al. 2020).

The United Nations Population Fund (UNFPA 2020) recently reported that the COVID-19 pandemic has had a grave impact on the health of women on a global scale. Although various health authorities all over the globe are battling to prevent the COVID-19 pandemic from having severe consequences for women's health, there have been unavoidable consequences. This is not surprising, as other vital services had been suspended and deferred due to the spread of the coronavirus.

Although COVID-19 has tended to more severely affect men, as direct caregivers who comprise over 60% of Africa's health workforce and essential social service providers, women in Africa are more directly exposed to the virus (Chuku et al. 2020). Women's domestic workload has also drastically increased due to school closures and the special needs of elderly relatives. Research in the Ebola outbreak has demonstrated that women suffered greater economic losses (Nkangu et al. 2017), and due to their concentration in the informal economy, women have been at higher risk of losing their jobs and income amid lockdowns during the current pandemic (Chuku et al. 2020; Forsyth 2020).

A UNFPA (2020) report indicates that the coronavirus outbreak has severely disrupted access to sexual and reproductive health and gender-based violence services; they project that 47 million women in low- and middle-income countries will lack access to modern contraceptives domestic abuse killings over a six-month lockdown period, gender-based violence will increase by 31 million, and 13 million additional child marriages will occur. Since the onset of COVID-19, there has been a dramatic spike in the number of people conducting online searches for help with domestic violence and sexual harassment in Africa, and in Kenya, calls for help against domestic violence have increased by 34% since lockdowns were imposed (Chuku et al. 2020). African women's organisations working to spread awareness and distribute masks and other equipment cite a lack of women's access to coronavirus information and unequal decision-making capacity as critical factors that could exacerbate the pandemic's impact on women and girls (Forsyth 2020).

In the UK, although the Home Secretary has pledged £3 million towards helplines for domestic violence victims who need support during this epidemic, some groups of women will be unable to benefit from this service due to their compromised immigration status partners, which leaves them vulnerable to deportation if they report their abusers. In many cases, the abuse that these women experience is psychological rather than physical, particularly in cases when abusers who have right to remain or other settled status are withholding money and threatening to report them, should they report their abuse. Some partners also punish their partners by withholding money. Many Black and Minority Ethnic (BAME) individuals also experience health challenges that make them particularly vulnerable to coronavirus. Recent analyses have shown that 61% of UK health workers who have died with COVID-19 and 33% of critically ill coronavirus patients are from BAME backgrounds (Intensive Care National Audit and Research Centre 2020; Marsh and McIntyre 2020.

WORKING TOGETHER FOR GENDER EQUALITY

Considering the culture and traditional set up of most African countries, women are the accelerators of the economy; if they are not given the opportunity to showcase their abilities regarding the economic growth may not be achieved as expected. Women play a crucial role in African economies as participants in the labour force as well as through unpaid labour in homes and gardens; however, gender inequality has been demonstrated to reduce economic growth in poor and developing countries in Africa compared with developed countries that have embraced equality in their economies

(Fosu 2017). The morality behind the eradication of inequality for the African woman is that more equality and opportunities for the women will open up and present the African race as an enlightened and diverse culture. Perceiving and treating women as inherently weaker and inferior beings has resulted in drastic consequences for gender and labour inequality (Mills 2017), which in the case of Africa has constrained the region's social and economic growth and sustainability. The reduction of gender-based inequalities in African societies will provide a major boost to the region's economic growth and stability (Udanoh and Zouria 2018).

Achieving SDG5 requires assessing gender inequalities and gender-based discrimination as well as focusing on policy changes in societies of origin and promoting the opportunities offered by migration for women and girls. McKinsey's report on the polio eradication effort described the implementation of a 'War Room Approach' whereby national and international organisational leaders met regularly 'to develop and execute eradication strategies, improve vaccination campaigns, and respond immediately to outbreaks'. The fight for gender equality requires a similar multidimensional, intersectional and long-term effort between governments, organisations, and the private sector with a singular focus on uplifting all women in politics, in the workplace and across social strata. Major efforts towards gender equality are represented by the 2004 Solemn Declaration on Gender Equality in Africa and the more recent adoption of the African Union strategy on

Gender Equality and Women's Empowerment (African Union 2004, 2019). However, for the call for gender inequality to succeed, there must be a change of perception, culture and education to help people change their attitudes towards financial responsibility. Financial responsibility should not be subject to gender considerations; rather, it should be universally perceived as a means to better lives for both men and the women around the world (Wale and Makina 2017).

REFERENCES

Gender attitudes and violence against women- Melinda R. York, 2011

ABANTU for Development. (2020). ABANTU as an organization. Retrieved from https://abantu-rowa.com/our-mission/

Adejugbe, A. and Adejugbe, A. (2018, 20 August). Women and discrimination in the workplace: a Nigerian perspective. Retrieved from http://dx.doi.org/10.2139/ssrn.3244971

African Union (2004). Solemn declaration on gender equality in Africa. Retrieved from https://www.un.org/en/africa/osaa/pdf/au/declaration_gender_equality_2004.pdf

African Union. (2019 February). African Union strategy on gender equality and women's empowerment 2018–2028. Retrieved from https://au.int/sites/default/files/documents/36195-doc-au_strategy_for_gender_equality_womens_empowerment_2018-2028_report.pdf

African Women's Development Fund. (2020). History. Retrieved from https://awdf.org/history-2/

Beattie, C. and Stevens, M.F. (2013). Married women and the law in premodern northwest Europe. Woodbridge, Suffolk, UK: Boydell Press.

Beyene, A.S., Chojenta, C., Roba, H.S., Melka, A.S. and Loxton, D.

(2019). Gender-based violence among female youths in educational institutions of Sub-Saharan Africa: a systematic review and meta-analysis. *Systematic Reviews*, 8, 59. https://doi.org/10.1186/s13643-019-0969-9

Canaday, M. (2008). 'Heterosexuality as a legal regime'. In M. Grossberg and C. L. Tomlins (eds.). *The Twentieth Century and after (1920—). The Cambridge History of Law in America*. 3. Cambridge, UK: Cambridge University Press.

Central Bureau of Statistics (CBS) and UNICEF Sudan. (2016). *Multiple indicator cluster survey 2014 of Sudan, final report*. Khartoum, Sudan: UNICEF and Central Bureau of Statistics (CBS). Retrieved from https://mics-surveys-prod.s3.amazonaws.com/MICS5/Middle%20East%20and%20North%20Africa/Sudan/2014/Final/Sudan%202014%20MICS_English.pdf

Central Statistical Agency/CSA/Ethiopia and ICF. 2016. *Ethiopia demographic and health survey 2016*. Addis Ababa, Ethiopia, and Rockville, Maryland, USA: CSA and ICF. Retrieved from https://dhsprogram.com/publications/publication-fr328-dhs-final-reports.cfm

Centre for Democracy and Development. (2018). Women in elective offices in Nigeria. Retrieved from https://www.africaportal.org/publications/women-elective-offices-nigeria/

Chuku, C., Mukasa, A. and Yenice, Y. (2020, 08 May). Putting women and girls' safety first in Africa's response to COVID-19. The Brookings Institution. Retrieved from https://www.brookings.edu/blog/africa-in-focus/2020/05/08/putting-women-and-girls-safety-first-in-africas-response-to-covid-19/

Copley, A. Decker, A. and Delavelle, F. (2020, 08 May). Supporting African women through the economic consequences of COVID-19. *Africa Can End Poverty*. Retrieved from https://blogs.worldbank.org/africacan/supporting-african-women-through-economic-consequences-covid-19

Cuberes, D. and Teignier, M. (2012). *Gender inequality and economic growth*. Washington, DC: World Bank.

Custer, J. A., The three waves of married women's property acts in the nineteenth century with a focus on Mississippi, New York, and Oregon (2013). 40 Ohio N.U. L. Rev. 395 (2014) ; Saint Louis U. Legal Studies Research Paper No. 2013-21. Retrieved from https://law.onu.edu/sites/default/files/395%20-%20Custer.pdf

Equal Measures 2030. Retrieved from https://data.em2030.org/wp-content/uploads/2019/07/EM2030_2019_Global_Report_English_WEB.pdf

Executive Committee of the High Commissioner's Programme (2006, 6 October). *Conclusion on women and girls at risk no. 105 (LVII) – 2006*, No. 105 (LVII), available at: https://www.refworld.org/docid/45339d922.html

Ferrand, F. (2008). *National report: France*. Commission of European Family Law. Retrieved from http://ceflonline.net/wp-content/uploads/France-Parental-Responsibilities.pdf

Forsyth, M. (2020, 03 April). Lessons from African feminists mobilizing against COVID-19. Earth Institute, Columbia University. Retrieved from https://blogs.ei.columbia.edu/2020/04/03/african-feminists-mobilizing-covid-19/

Fosu, A.K. (2017). Growth, inequality, and poverty reduction in developing countries: Recent global evidence. *Research in Economics*, 71(2), 306-336.

Hakura, D., Hussain, M., Newiak, M., Thakoor, V. and Yang F. (2016). *Inequality, gender gaps and economic growth: comparative evidence for Sub-Saharan Africa*. IMF Working Paper 16/111. Retrieved from https://www.imf.org/external/pubs/ft/wp/2016/wp16111.pdf

Intensive Care National Audit and Research Centre. (2020, 15 May). *ICNARC report on COVID-19 in critical care*. Retrieved from https://www.icnarc.org/DataServices/Attachments/Download/cbcb6217-f698-ea11-9125-00505601089b

International Labour Organization. (2018). Women and men in the informal economy: A statistical picture. 3rd ed. Retrieved from https://www.ilo.org/global/publications/books/WCMS_626831/

lang--en/index.htm

Kenya National Bureau of Statistics (2015). *Kenya demographic and health survey 2014*. Rockville, MD, USA: Kenya National Bureau of Statistics, Ministry of Health/Kenya, National AIDS Control Council/Kenya, Kenya Medical Research Institute, National Council for Population and Development/Kenya, and ICF International. Retrieved from https://dhsprogram.com/publications/publication-fr308-dhs-final-reports.cfm

Marsh, S. and McIntyre, M. (2020 25 May). Six in 10 UK health workers killed by Covid-19 are BAME. *The Guardian*. Retrieved from https://www.theguardian.com/world/2020/may/25/six-in-10-uk-health-workers-killed-by-covid-19-are-bame

Mills, M.B. (2017). Gendered morality tales: discourses of gender, labour, and value in globalising Asia. *The Journal of Development Studies*, 53(3), 316-330, DOI: 10.1080/00220388.2016.1184251

Ministère du Plan et Suivi de la Mise en œuvre de la Révolution de la Modernité [MPSMRM/Congo], Ministère de la Santé Publique [MSP/Congo] and ICF International. (2014). *Enquête démographique et de santé en République Démocratique du Congo 2013-2014*. Rockville, Maryland, USA: MPSMRM, MSP, and ICF International. Retrieved from https://dhsprogram.com/

publications/publication-fr300-dhs-final-reports.cfm

Ministry of Health and National Bureau of Statistics (2010). *South Sudan household survey 2010, final report*. Juba, South Sudan. Retrieved from https://mics.unicef.org/surveys

National Bureau of Statistics (2017). *Labour force statistics vol. 2: employment by sector report*. Retrieved from https://nigerianstat.gov.ng/download/711

National Bureau of Statistics (NBS) and United Nations Children's Fund (UNICEF). (2017) *Multiple indicator cluster survey 2016-17, survey findings report*. Abuja, Nigeria: National Bureau of Statistics and United Nations Children's Fund.

National Population Commission (NPC) [Nigeria] and ICF International (2014). *Nigeria demographic and health survey 2013*. Abuja, Nigeria, and Rockville, Maryland, USA: NPC and ICF International.

Nkangu, M.N., Olatunde, O.A. & Yaya, S. (2017). The perspective of gender on the Ebola virus using a risk management and population health framework: a scoping review. Infectious Diseases of Poverty, 6, 135. https://doi.org/10.1186/s40249-017-0346-7

Obiukwu, O. (2019, 22 September). Gender equality: Nigeria must mind the wide gap. *New African*. Retrieved from https://newafricanmagazine.com/19891/

Okeke, T.C., Anyaehie, U.S.B. and Ezenyeaku, C.C.K. (2012). An overview of female genital mutilation in Nigeria. *Annals of Medical and Health Science Research*, 2(1), 70–73. Retrieved from www.ncbi.nlm.nih.gov/pmc/articles/PMC3507121

Olarewaju, (2019, 06 March). Nigerian women entrepreneurs draw the short straw on education levels. *The Conversation*. Retrieved from https://theconversation.com/nigerian-women-entrepreneurs-draw-the-short-straw-on-education-levels-112843

Perry, S. (2002). *Aspects of contemporary France*. London: Routledge.

Ramirez, F., Soysal, Y. and Shanahan, S. (1997). The changing logic of political citizenship: cross-national acquisition of women's suffrage rights, 1890 to 1990. *American Sociological Review*, 62(5), 735-745. Retrieved from www.jstor.org/stable/2657357

Randriamaro, Z. (2012). *Greening the economy and increasing economic equity for women farmers in Madagascar*. Policy Research Brief 34, International Policy Centre for Inclusive Growth. Retrieved from http://www.ipc-undp.org/pub/IPCPolicyResearchBrief34.pdf

Ridgeway, C.L. (2011). *Framed by gender: how gender inequality persists in the modern world*. Oxford: Oxford University Press.

Ruro, S.J. (2009). Sexual abuse of school age children: evidence from Kenya. *Journal of International Cooperation in Education*, 12(1), 177– 192

Teignier, M. and Cuberes, D. (2014). *Aggregate costs of gender gaps in the labour market: a quantitative estimate.* UB Economics Working Papers 2014/308. Retrieved from http://www.ub.edu/ubeconomics/wp-content/uploads/2014/02/308-Web.pdf

Udanoh, M.U. and Zouria, A. (2018). Using gender inequality to predict the rate of African women entrepreneurship. *International Journal of Emerging Trends in Social Sciences*, 3(1), 17-28.

Uganda Bureau of Statistics and ICF. (2018). *Uganda demographic and health survey 2016*. Kampala, Uganda and Rockville, Maryland, USA: UBOS and ICF. Retrieved from https://dhsprogram.com/pubs/pdf/FR333/FR333.pdf

UNESCO Institute for Statistics (2016). *Leaving no one behind: How far on the way to universal primary and secondary education*? Global Education Monitoring Report: Policy Paper, 27. Retrieved from https://unesdoc.unesco.org/ark:/48223/pf0000245238

UNESCO Institute for Statistics (2020). World inequality database

on education: Nigeria. Retrieved from https://www.education-inequalities.org/countries/nigeria#?
dimension=sex&group=all&year=latest '

United Nations Children's Fund (2014). Ending child marriage: progress and prospects. New York: UNICEF. Retrieved from https://www.unicef.org/media/files/
Child_Marriage_Report_7_17_LR.pdf

UNICEF (2016). Female genital mutilation/cutting: A global concern. Retrieved from https://data.unicef.org/wp-content/uploads/2016/04/FGMC-2016-brochure_250.pdf

UNICEF Kenya Country Office, Division of Violence Prevention, National Center for Injury Prevention and Control, U.S. Centers for Disease Control and Prevention, Kenya National Bureau of Statistics. (2012). Violence against children in Kenya: findings from a 2010 national survey. Retrieved at https://www.unicef.org/esaro/VAC_in_Kenya.pdf

UNICEF Uganda (2013). *Assessing child protection, safety and security issues for children in Ugandan primary and secondary schools*. Research Briefing. Kampala: UNICEF Uganda.

United Nations Population Fund. (2020, 27 April). *Impact of the COVID-19 pandemic on family planning and ending gender-based violence, female genital mutilation and child marriage*. Retrieved from https://www.unfpa.org/resources/impact-covid-19-pandemic-family-planning-and-ending-gender-based-violence-female-genital

United Nations Women (2016a). Prevalence data on different forms of violence against women. Retrieved from https://evaw-global-database.unwomen.org/en/countries

United Nations Women (2016a). Progress of the world's women 2015-2016. Retrieved from https://progress.unwomen.org/en/2015/pdf/UNW_progressreport.pdf

Vogelstein, R. (2016). How women's participation in conflict prevention and resolution advances US interests. Washington, DC: CFR. Retrieved from https://www.cfr.org/report/how-womens-participation-conflict-prevention-and-resolution-advances-us-interests

Wale, L.E. and Makina, D. (2017). Account ownership and use of financial services among individuals: Evidence from selected Sub-Saharan African economies. *African Journal of Economic and Management Studies*, 8(1), 19-35. https://doi.org/10.1108/AJEMS-03-2017-146

Weker, R. (2016). '"Who belongs" or the question of women's citizenship in Switzerland since 1798. In S.L. Kimble and M. Röwekamp (eds), *New perspectives on European women's legal history*. Routledge Research in Gender and History. London: Routledge.

Wodon, Quentin T.; Male, Chata; Onagoruwa, Adenike Opeoluwa; Yedan, Ali. 2017. *Key findings ahead of the October 2017 high level meeting on ending child marriage in West and Central Africa* (English). *Girls' education and child marriage in West and Central Africa*. Washington, D.C. : World Bank Group. http://documents.worldbank.org/curated/en/429021508525003676/ Key-findings-ahead-of-the-October-2017-high-level-meeting-on- ending-child-marriage-in-West-and-Central-Africa

Woetzal, J., Madgavkar, A., Ellingrud, K., Labaye, E., Devillard, S. Kutcher, E., Manyika, J., Dobbs, R. and Krishnan, M. (2015). *How advancing women's equality can add $12 trillion to global growth*. New York: McKinsey and Company. Retrieved from https://www.mckinsey.com/~/media/McKinsey/Featured%20Insights/ Employment%20and%20Growth/How%20advancing%20womens% 20equality%20can%20add%2012%20trillion%20to%20global% 20growth/MGI%20Power%20of%20parity_Full% 20report_September%202015.ashx

World Data Lab (2020). World poverty clock. Retrieved from https://worldpoverty.io/map

World Economic Forum (2019). *The global gender gap report 2020*. Retrieved from http://www3.weforum.org/docs/ WEF_GGGR_2020.pdf

World Health Organization (2018). Female genital mutilation.

Retrieved from https://www.who.int/news-room/fact-sheets/detail/ female-genital-mutilation

World Health Organization (2019). Maternal health in Nigeria: generating information for action. Retrieved from https:// www.who.int/reproductivehealth/maternal-health-nigeria/en/

2

GENDER INEQUALITY AND
CAREER ASPIRATIONS

Sophia Aluko

INTRODUCTION

Multiple explanations have been provided for gender inequality in the workplace. In some quarters, there is a perception that women are less ambitious than men and less suited to the competitive environment that characterises much of the corporate world. Some have postulated that women are biologically wired to be nurturers, which makes them better suited to stay in the home and care for the family.

It is worth taking a step back in early human history and examining how we evolved to understand the root cause of this perception of fixed division of labour between the genders. Researchers into origins and development of early humans have long believed that during the new early age (about 12,000 years ago) men were the hunters who left the comfort of the cave to confront dangerous animals and work under hostile conditions in order to provide food for the family and tribe, whereas women remained to look after the children and gathered foods and crops near home.

However, earlier assumptions about fixed divisions of labour and gender roles among our early ancestors have been challenged by the recent discovery of the remains of female hunters at South American archaeological sites. This finding suggests that work roles were not binary during early human history; rather, any available able-bodied individual would perform the tasks necessary to sustain the tribe.[1]

Although it has become apparent that our understanding of the history of gender roles and divisions of labour is far from accurate, these ideas have long been accepted as the norm and continue to shape how we think about gender roles until this very day. Although women comprise half of the world's population, they remain under-represented in senior positions where critical decisions are made and are overrepresented in lower paying jobs. Even highly educated women are more likely than men to undertake unpaid care jobs, are over three times more likely to work part-time, are less likely to progress in work, and tend to be employed in lower paying industries and occupations [2]

This article examines some of the historical and social factors contributing to gender inequality in the workforce and provides some ideas and proposals to address the current issues.

APPROACH

This study examines gender inequality from the lens of socio-cultural norms and beliefs. Specifically, it considers the ways that Western values have shaped gender roles and divisions of labour. It is an established fact that norms, rules, and beliefs underpin how we think, feel, act and behave, which shapes our worldview and consequently our perception and expectations of gender roles.

FINDINGS

The challenges that limit women's career aspirations begin at the point of birth. In many cultures, females have served as the primary carers who look after the home and children while males work outside the home and financially provide for the family. This traditional allocation of unpaid domestic responsibilities to women has played a strong role in preserving the status quo in the workforce.

Gender roles in the UK were firmly established by the beginning of the second Industrial Revolution during the mid-19th century, when men assumed supervisory roles while women and children worked in a domestic capacity or earned meagre wages on the factory floor. At the same time, the expansion of European colonialism spread Western gender role norms to other parts of the world. In many of these societies, this resulted in minimal disruption, as men's roles were outside the home and in the public sphere, such as in government and commerce, whereas women participated in the private sphere of the home. However, placing gender roles in neat boxes did not align with customs in many parts of Africa and Latin America, where women participated in the public sphere as traders and merchants.[3]

Over a hundred years after the first Industrial Revolution, women's roles had changed very little. Following the Second World War, there was a surge in demand for labour; however, so many men had been tragically killed in the war that women were needed to take up jobs in industries and government. However, these roles were primarily limited to junior-level secretarial and clerical positions, whereas men occupied the managerial or supervisory roles. This set up hasn't changed very much in present times with increasing number of women working part-time and in low-paying jobs despite often having high levels of education.

We are beginning to see some progress; however, strong barriers continue to undermine gender equality. Women are playing a more active role in the workplace, entering once male-dominated occupations, and occupying senior roles such as CEOs of large organisations, business owners and senior officials in the public sector. However, the few women who manage to ascend to these positions have publicly shared the juggling act required to combine home and work responsibilities. Some of these challenges are associated with being the 'only woman' in the room and feelings of guilt when they need to prioritise work over family needs. Men typically do not experience the same dilemmas, as society expects men to occupy such roles and has therefore ensured that supportive structures are available to enable them to succeed in high-level positions.

In 2018, women occupied 48% of entry-level jobs, which is nearly an even split; however, there is a significant decline in their representation at the managerial level. Disparities are particularly stark at the most senior, c-suite roles, where women represent just 22% of executive personnel. The numbers are even more abysmal for women of colour, who occupy only 17% of entry-level roles and 4% of c-suite positions.[4]

Women are particularly underrepresented in leadership roles between the ages of 28-35 years, which coincides with their reproductive years. When women leave the workplace to start a family, the cost and barriers of re-entering the workforce are high, and not many are fortunate to return to work. In the UK, the average cost of childcare for an infant under two years of age is £1,008 per month; however, the average pre-tax income only slightly exceeds that amount at £1,272 per month.[5] Thus, childcare is unaffordable for most families even when both parents are engaged in full time employment. As the primary carers, women are often obliged to make a trade-off between spending all their income to pay for childcare or taking on those responsibilities and forfeiting income from paid employment.

And as a result, we are seeing a trend where some women delay childbirth until they are financially comfortable and have progressed to more senior positions and can afford the high cost of childcare.

However, we are seeing that women in countries in Africa and Asia are not having to make these trade-offs. When they re-enter the workplace after childbirth, they are able to progress up the ranks faster than their counterparts in the West. But worth stating that affordable childcare and an extended family support networks are contributing to lowering the barriers to re-entering the labour market.

CONCLUSION: INTERVENTIONS TO REDUCE GENDER GAPS IN THE LABOUR MARKET

There is a very clear business case for actively promoting gender equality. A recent report reveals that reducing gender gaps in labour market participation, science, technology, engineering and maths (STEM) qualifications, and wages could increase the size of the UK economy by approximately 2%, or £55 billion, by 2030.[6]

We have seen a number of actions undertaken by governments and businesses to close the gender gap in the labour market; however, much still needs to be done. Childcare costs in the UK remain stubbornly high compared with the EU. Although the UK government offers a subsidy to offset childcare cost, it is not sufficient to encourage women in the early stages of their careers or working low-paying jobs to return to work. Although Britain has left the EU and is no longer bound by its laws, it can borrow ideas from countries in Scandinavia, where childcare costs are heavily subsidised, which has led to more gender equality in the labour market.

Equally, men should not be constrained by societal expectations and should be offered more generous paternity leave that will encourage them to remain home and care for their new-born infants. Men should not be made to feel inadequate for taking extended time away from work to look after their children, which will enable their partners to return to work sooner should they desire to do so.

For equality to be achieved in the workplace, we must also ensure that it is socially acceptable for women to be the primary breadwinners of the household. High-earning women should be acknowledged and celebrated rather than perceived as emasculating their partners. The notion of fixed gender roles at home and in the workplace should be actively discouraged through education and reinforcing the message that everyone should be free to fulfil their aspirations, whatever those might be, rather than being encumbered by societal expectations.

To some degree, the COVID-19 pandemic has created more opportunities to achieve equality in the workplace. The pandemic has disrupted every area of our lives, including engendering unprecedented trends that have the potential to change how we work. Most people who can work from home have been doing so since the pandemic with hybrid working now becoming the norm.

Although women appear to be bearing the brunt of childcare responsibilities, we are seeing reports that men are becoming more involved in raising their children than during any time in historical memory, which is a silver lining that should be encouraged as we navigate a post-pandemic world.

As hybrid working is now the norm for most office-based roles, I remain hopeful that with the flexibility that hybrid working offer, more women will take on more responsibilities that will enable them to progress in their careers, and those who have taken time off for childcare purposes can re-enter the workforce without being obliged to spend hours away from their families.

The workplace of the future must offer the flexibility to attract and retain top talent regardless of gender. In order to achieve this, home life must be considered paramount, and travelling hours from home to work in an office building in the city centre will no longer be a yardstick for career progression. If governments and businesses embrace these new ways of working, then more women will be able to achieve their career aspirations and occupy roles that had previously been out of their reach, and we might hopefully see a marked reduction in gender inequality.

REFERENCES

Wei-Has, M. 2020. Prehistoric female hunter discovery upends gender role assumptions. https://www.nationalgeographic.com/science/2020/11/prehistoric-female-hunter-discovery-upends-gender-role-assumptions/#

The World Bank. 2019. Population, female (% of total population). https://data.worldbank.org/indicator/SP.POP.TOTL.FE.ZS

World History Project. 2021. Changing gender roles. https://www.khanacademy.org/humanities/whp-1750/xcabef9ed3fc7da7b:unit-4-labor-and-society/xcabef9ed3fc7da7b:4-3-gender/a/read-changing-gender-roles-beta

Ziv, S. 2021. 7 striking facts about the state of women in the workplace. https://www.themuse.com/advice/7-striking-facts-women-in-the-workplace-2018#:~:text=In%202018%2C%20women%20made%20up,%25%20of%20C%2Dsuite%20executives.

The Money Advice Service. 2021. Average childcare costs. https://www.moneyadviceservice.org.uk/en/articles/childcare-costs

Government Equalities Office. 2019 *Gender equality at every stage: A roadmap for change.* https://assets.publishing.service.gov.uk/government/uploads/system/uploads/attachment_data/file/821889/GEO_GEEE_Strategy_Gender_Equality_Roadmap_Rev_1__1_.pdf

BIOGRAPHY

Sophia Aluko

Sophia Aluko is the founder of *The Steer Network*, a career and personal development organisation set up to empower professionals from diverse backgrounds to fulfil their personal and professional aspirations. She has over twenty years' experience in multiple sectors and has worked in various senior capacities in the commercial sector where she has been responsible for leading and implementing transformation and change.

She has lived and worked in different countries which enabled her to develop a deep appreciation of different cultures and why it is important to have diverse voices in decision making.

Sophia is passionate about gender equality and uses her platform to advocate for more gender balance across various sectors. She is also a Trustee of GFW UK a charity set up to advocate and promote gender diversity in the most disadvantaged communities. She holds a B.sc Hons in Insurance & Risk Management and an MBA from Imperial Business College, University of London. She is a qualified accountant with the Chartered Institute of Management Accountant.

3

A CASE FOR RE-ENACTING

GENDER-BASED VIOLENCE (GBV)

Ola-Kris Akinola

INTRODUCTION

When one of University of Cape Town's (UCT) students, Uyinene Mrwetyana, went missing on 24 August 2019, the entire nation braced for the worst. Sadly, on 2nd September, the South African Police Services (SAPS) confirmed her death. Like many South African young girls and women in past years, Uyinene was first raped before she was gruesomely murdered. Whereas this case and several others like it were major highlights of crime reportage and debates for the latter part of 2019, such stories have become the realities of females in South Africa.

PURPOSE

Studies of gender-based violence (GBV) have reported prevalence rates of gender-based violence ranging from

11.6% to 75.6% in sub-Saharan Africa, and rising incidents continue to negatively impact South African society. Survivors of sexual abuse, rape, and femicide experience immeasurable trauma and anger because they feel disappointed by a legal system that has failed to support and protect them. This book explores the question of whether and how applied theatre could play an integral role in changing the narrative of South Africa as the rape capital of the world.

DESIGN/METHODOLOGY/APPROACH

Through a narrative ethnographic account of how performances reveal the relational stories/selves of actors, I have highlighted the ability of theatre as a tool for counselling and psychological healing and demonstrate the potential of research cross-pollination to generate social change through the application of an ethnographic approach to a study of GBV and the dramatic arts. Specifically, through participant observation and face-to-face interviews, the study profiled the narratives of several first-level undergraduate acting students who had experienced GBV and had also cast as victims of sexual violence in *Ghost Twerkers*, a play that was written and produced with the aim of engaging with the on-going conversation concerning the GBV plague.

FINDINGS

Ken Plummer describes stories as 'documents of life'. In a similar vein, in his book Nation and Narration, Homi K. Bhabba corroborates that a nation's self-image is shaped and marked by the form and content of the stories it tells about itself. Consequently, stories of incidences of GBV in South Africa continue to negatively shape the country, marking some of its men as unconscionable and brutal.

In 2004, Amanda Stuart, an applied theatre specialist at Central, commenced an intervention whereby she considered theatrical enactments of stories of actual lived events. Thereafter, the challenge of dealing with trauma, a condition that resists articulation and cannot be assimilated to cognition and functioning (Lacan 1994, Caruth 1996), as a postponed or 'belated experience' was theatrically emanated.

Whether staged as a play before an audience or perpetrated in secret at homes or in dark corners in some remote part of the world, GBV has become an epidemic that must be defeated. For this reason, it is imperative to familiarise ourselves with and strive to help victims overcome the trauma of victims of gender abuse. Applied theatre practitioners ought to become more curious about whether through participation (acting), women who play victimised characters are able to overcome the stigma of having been real-life victims of sexual violence.

CONCLUSION

The findings highlight the ability of theatre as a tool for counselling and psychological healing. The findings can be used to provide counsellors with new tools to support individuals who have experienced sexual violence.

Keywords: gender-based violence; sexual violence; narrative ethnography; dramatic arts; trauma

REFERENCES

Bhabba, H.K. 1990. Nation and narration. London: Routledge.

Caruth, C. 1996. *Unclaimed experience: Trauma, narrative, and history*. Baltimore: Johns Hopkins University Press.

Lacan, J. and Sheridan, A. 1994. The four fundamental concepts of psychoanalysis.

Muluneh, M.D., Stulz, V., Francis, L., and Aghom, K. 2020. Gender based violence against women in sub-Saharan Africa: A systematic review and meta-analysis of cross-sectional studies. *International Journal of Environmental Research and Public Health* 17(3), 903. doi: 10.3390/ijerph17030903.

Plummer, K. 1983. Documents of life: An introduction to the problems and literature of a humanistic method. London: G. Allen & Unwin.

BIOGRAPHY

Ola-Kris Akinola

Akinola Christopher Ogungbemi PhD (also known as Ola-Kris), is a doctor in applied theatre, is an academic, dramatist, playwright, theatre administrator and Church planter. He has authored book chapters, poems, journal articles as well as written and premiered plays in Nigeria and South Africa, such as "Hakuna Matata" (2008), "Tsietsi" (2016), "The Prince of Sovenga"(2017), "The Serial Kisser and the Code of Silence" (2019). "Ghost Twerkers: a play on gender based violence (GBV)" was published by SOPHOS BOOKS, London, in March of 2022.

As an actor, he has featured in two South African movies: "Jacob's Cross" (2010-2016) and "Room 9" (2015), and as directed two Nollywood films: "The Dragons" (2012) and "The Lincoln's Clan" (2013). Dr Ola-Kris is a Senior Lecturer in Performing Arts at University of Limpopo, South Africa.

4

THE IMPACT OF GENDER-BASED VIOLENCE ON MENTAL HEALTH

'Lade Hephzibah Olugbemi

In this paper, I focus on the dynamics and impacts of domestic abuse and sexual assault as forms of gender-based violence (GBV) on the mental health of victims or survivors.

Global reports indicate that 35% of women have experienced some form of physical and/or sexual violence committed by an intimate partner or non-partner (World Health Organisation et al., 2013). Although attention towards GBV tends to be primarily focused on women, it can also be directed toward boys and men as well as non-binary and other gender non-conforming people. GBV can be experienced within family circles, communities, and organisations, with dire and long-lasting consequences that is trans-generational and cutting across culture and ethnicities.

In *Breaking the Barriers: Early Intervention to Mental Health Issues*, I discuss how life affects us all differently; however, certain factors can affect our mental health and influence how we think and respond to challenges and opportunities (Olugbemi, 2020). GBV is among many factors that can trigger mental health issues and illness. As the World Health Organisation (WHO, 2004) elaborates, *'mental health is a state of well-being in which the individual realises his or her own abilities, can cope with the normal stressors of life, can work productively and fruitfully, and is able to make a contribution to his or her community'*. From this definition, we can see that any act of violence, whether physical or emotional, can affect the ways that a person copes with the stressors of life, and GBV is in fact a perpetuating life stressor that can trigger deterioration in mental health if no appropriate psychological input is offered or sought after the violence or harm.

Although there have been manifold societal conversations about GBV, the primary focus tends to be more on the criminality of the act and the punishment of perpetrator, and the need to rehouse or resettle the victim or survivor. Much less attention has been devoted to understanding and ameliorating the negative psychosocial impacts on victims. However, GBV is a serious risk factor for mental health disorders, and individuals who have suffered intra familial, communal, or organisational abuse or female genital mutilation (FGM) often experience a trauma that they may not be able to voice, and when they do express their pain, the existing support systems are sometimes not adequate or sufficient to take them through the healing process.

DOMESTIC ABUSE

Domestic abuse can occur in the form of physical violence, sexual coercion, psychological abuse, financial, or stalking. According to the Committee on the Elimination of Discrimination against Women (CEDAW, 1992), domestic abuse is a gendered crime that is deeply rooted in the societal inequality between men and women. The Convention on the Elimination of All Forms of Discrimination against Women adopted by the UN General Assembly in 1979 defines GBV as a 'form of gender-based violence, violence directed against a woman because she is a woman or that affects women disproportionately'.

During the COVID-19 lockdowns, many women and girls around the world have been restricted to unsafe environments where they are at an increased risk of experiencing violence by an intimate partner or family member. Approximately one-third of women worldwide have experienced physical and/or sexual violence at the hands of an intimate partner, and 18% have experienced domestic violence in the past 12 months (United Nations Department of Economic and Social Affairs, 2020).

SEXUAL VIOLENCE

Sexual violence, which includes rape and other forms of sexual assault, is an act of physical, psychological, and emotional violation imposed in the form of the sexual act committed against an individual's will, and it can occur in intimate relationships or within communities. Sexual violence against girls and women is a growing trend, and the Covid-19 pandemic has only worsened its impact. One in four women experience rape at some point during their lifetime, and one in 30 men have also experienced a sexual assault (IDAS, 2021). These are startling statistic that needs to generate more action across international governmental structure. According to Wyatt et al. (2017), sexual violence has become a critical and ubiquitous form of gender-based violence across Africa, where innocent Black African girls are being kidnapped and raped at alarmingly high rates. Reports are the In Nigeria, there have been several substantiated reports of the mayhem that the Boko Haram religious militants have unleashed on several villages in the northern part of the country whereas part of their conquest, they have abducted women as sex slaves and married them off to their war leaders. Sexual and other forms of gender-based violence are common in conflict settings and are known risk factors for mental health and psychosocial wellbeing.

Armed conflict has been recorded in 153 locations since the end of World War II. There have been 248 armed conflicts documented. It is important to note that sexual violence has long been part of armed conflicts, with remarkable variation as to scale, type of violence, who is targeted and the extent to which there exists a specific tactic to commit such violence.

It is pertinent to note that the World Report on Violence and Health (WRVH) defines sexual violence and gender-based violence separately. According to WRVH, sexual violence is defined as *"any sexual act, attempt to obtain a sexual act, unwanted sexual comments or advances, or acts to traffic, or otherwise directed, against a person's sexuality using coercion, by any person regardless of their relationship to the victim, in any setting, including but not limited to home and work"*. GBV is defined in broader umbrella term referring to *"any harmful act that is perpetrated against a person's will, and that is based on socially ascribed (gender) differences between males and females, which in most settings privilege men."* Rates of sexual and other forms of gender-based violence are reported to be higher in areas of armed conflict than in non-conflict affected settings

Sexual assault negatively impacts the physical and mental health of both female and male victims. The health consequences of sexual assault include physical to psychological effects ranging from temporary and sometimes chronic disorders. Moreover, victims of sexual violence may not be able to voice their experiences to others, which opens the door for mental health problems to grow and thrive.

PSYCHOLOGICAL CONSEQUENCES OF SEXUAL ASSAULT
IN WOMEN

Comparative research has identified a wide range of short- and long-term mental health problems among victims of rape, which vary from person to person. Short-term effects of sexual abuse include:

◆ Depression

◆ Post-Traumatic Stress Disorder (PTSD)

◆ Rape Trauma Syndrome

◆ Anxiety

◆ Battered women syndrome

◆ Social Phobias

◆ Increased substance use

◆ Suicidal ideation

◆ Psychosis

◆ Feelings of shame or guilt

◆ Social withdrawal

In cases of long-term effects of sexual harassment, victims may experience:

- Chronic headaches

- Fatigue

- Sleep disturbances (nightmares or flashbacks)

- Recurrent nausea

- Eating disorders

- Menstrual pain

- Sexual difficulties

STATISTICS

A survey conducted by the National Women's Study Association collected data on rape prevalence as well as detailing devastating mental health impacts on victims. The findings include that nearly one-third (31%) of rape victims had developed PTSD and 30% experienced depression (Kessler et al., 2017). According to the National Intimate Partner and Sexual Violence Survey, 19.3% of women in the USA had been raped in their lifetime (Oram, 2019). The European Union's Fundamental Rights Survey found that 5% (9 million) women in Europe had been raped since the age of 15 and over 0.8% (1.5 million) had been raped at some point during in the past few months preceding the study (Oshodi et al., 2016).

IMPACT OF DOMESTIC ABUSE ON VICTIM'S MENTAL HEALTH

Domestic violence can result in shame, confusion and fear, which may manifest in insomnia, anxiety, depression, or PTSD. Psychological abuse has been linked to social isolation both for adult victims and their children (Goodman & Smyth, 2011; Naughton et al., 2020). Rates of PTSD among women who have experienced physical domestic violence have been found to be considerably higher than those among general community samples of women, ranging from 31% to 84%, (Golding, 1999), and many victims feel helpless and in danger even long after the last victimisation event (Salcioglu, 2017). Women who experience domestic violence are also more likely to experience chronic depression, with symptoms continuing for months or even years after they are no longer living under abusive conditions (Vampbell and Soeken, 1999). It is important to note that victims who experience mental health challenges because of GBV are three times more likely to have suicidal thoughts or completed suicide (Aitken and Munro, 2018). GBV refers to psychological, physical, or sexual harm committed against an individual against their will. The impacts include undermined confidence, physical disabilities, stigma, and shame. Sexual violence also puts women at increased risk of HIV/AIDS.

RECOMMENDATIONS

A great deal of work remains to be done within African communities to support victims of gender-based violence, including domestic violence victims and sexual assault victims. More works needs to be done to assist victims of sexual violence in war zones. Refugee camps, and camps for internally displaced persons (IDP) need to be equipped with more psychosocial support for victims.

Community leaders need to be trained on how to offer support, and front line workers need to be trained on how to respond to those who have been affected. The Mental Health First Aid training comes to mind as a skill acquisition resource that all community leaders need. Local, regional and national organisations can continue stepping up their efforts, and international organisations such as the WHO need to be encouraged to set up hubs in African countries that can provide psychosocial support to victims of gender-based violence.

REFERENCES

Campbell, J.C. & Soeken, K.L. (1999). Women's responses to battering over time: An analysis of change. *Journal of Interpersonal Violence*,14, 21–40.

Golding, J.M. (1999). Intimate partner violence as a risk factor for mental disorders: A meta-analysis. *Journal of Family Violence*, 14, 99–132.

Goodman, L. A., & Smyth, K. F. (2011). A call for a social network-oriented approach to services for survivors of intimate partner violence. *Psychology of Violence*, 1(2), 79. doi: org/10.1037/a0022977

IDAS (2021). Facts About rape. Available at: https://www.idas.org.uk/our-services/sexual-violence/facts-about-rape/

Jewkes R, Sen P, Garcia-Moreno C: Chapter 6. Sexual Violence. World Report on Violence and Health. Edited by: Krug EG, Dahlberg LL, Mercy JA, Zwi AB, Lozano R. 2002, Geneva, Switzerland: WHO

Kessler, R., Aguilar-Gaxiola, S., Alonso, J., Benjet, C., Bromet, E., & Cardoso, G. et al. (2017). Trauma and PTSD in the WHO World Mental Health Surveys. *European Journal of Psychotraumatology*, *8* (sup5), 1353383. https://doi.org/10.1080/20008198.2017.1353383

Naughton, C. M., O'Donnell, A. T., & Muldoon, O. T. (2020). Exposure to Domestic violence and abuse: Evidence of distinct physical and psychological dimensions. Journal of interpersonal violence, 35(15-16), 3102–3123. https://doi.org/10.1177/0886260517706763

Olugbemi, L.H. (2020). *Breaking the Barriers: Early intervention to mental health issues.*

Oram, S. (2019). Sexual violence and mental health. *Epidemiology And Psychiatric Sciences*, *28*(6), 592-593. https://doi.org/10.1017/s2045796019000106

Oshodi, Y., Macharia, M., Lachman, A., & Seedat, S. (2016). Immediate and long-term mental health outcomes in adolescent female rape survivors. *Journal of Interpersonal Violence*, *35*(1-2), 252-267. https://doi.org/10.1177/0886260516682522

Prather, C., Fuller, T., Jeffries, W., Marshall, K., Howell, A., Belyue-Umole, A., & King, W. (2018). Racism, African American women, and their sexual and reproductive health: A review of historical and contemporary evidence and implications for health equity. *Health Equity*, *2*(1), 249-259. https://doi.org/10.1089/heq.2017.0045

Salcioglu, E., Urhan, S., Pirinccioglu, T., & Aydin, S. (2017). Anticipatory fear and helplessness predict PTSD and depression in domestic violence survivors. *Psychological Trauma: Theory, Research, Practice, and Policy,* 9(1), 117–125. https://doi.org/10.1037/tra0000200

Themner L, Wallensteen P: Armed conflicts, 1946–2010. J Peace Res. 2011, 48 (4): 525-536. 10.1177/0022343311415302

United Nations Committee on the Elimination of Discrimination Against Women. CEDAW General Recommendation No. 19: Violence against women, 1992. Available at: https://www.refworld.org/docid/52d920c54.html

United Nations Department of Economic and Social Affairs (2020). The world's women 2020: Trends and statistics. Available at: https://www.un.org/en/desa/world%E2%80%99s-women-2020

United Nations General Assembly (1979). Convention on the Elimination of All Forms of Discrimination against Women. Available at: https://www.un.org/womenwatch/daw/cedaw/cedaw.htm

Wood EJ: Sexual violence during war: explaining variation. Order, Conflict and Violence Conference. 2004, New Haven, CT: Yale University

World Health Organisation (2021). Mental health: strengthening our response. https://www.who.int/news-room/fact-sheets/detail/mental-health-strengthening-our-response

World Health Organization, Department of Reproductive Health and Research, London School of Hygiene and Tropical Medicine, South African Medical Research Council (2013). *Global and regional estimates of violence against women: prevalence and health effects of intimate partner violence and non-partner sexual violence.* Available at: http://www.who.int/reproductivehealth/publications/violence/9789241564625/en/

Wyatt, G., Davhana-Maselesele, M., Zhang, M., Wong, L., Nicholson, F., & Sarkissian, A. et al. (2017). A longitudinal study of the aftermath of rape among rural South African women. *Psychological Trauma: Theory, Research, Practice, And Policy*, 9(3), 309-316. https://doi.org/10.1037/tra0000246

BIOGRAPHY

'Lade Hephzibah Olugbemi

'**Lade Hephzibah Olugbemi** BA, LLB, LLM is a lawyer and a manager working at one of the Local Authorities in London, United Kingdom. She graduated from the Ondo State University, Nigeria in 1987 with a degree in English Language. She went back to University after 16 years in 2003 to study a profession she had always wanted to study, Law. She obtained her LLB in 2007 from the University of Wolverhampton, specialising in Business and Commercial Law. Her passion for mental health motivated her to study further and she proceeded to enroll for the Masters in Law. Her major was in Human Right Law with a deep slant of study on the rights of the vulnerable persons under the Mental Health Acts. She completed her LLM with distinction in 2009. Her passion and natural instinctive flair to advocate for people especially patients or service users that have had reasons to be in the health and social care sector was generated when she worked as a support worker in organisations that worked with people with challenges living independently. 'Lade is the CEO of The NOUS Charity Incorporated Organisation, a registered not for profit organisation raising awareness through workshops, seminars and community work. She is also a Mental Health First Aid Instructor and she delivers mental first aid training in the communities. 'Lade will like to see policies changed reflecting the needs of the Black, Asian and Minority Ethnic in the UK. Lade's work is not only limited to the UK,, Lade has conducted workshops and conferences in Nigeria, She is the CEO of the Nous Foundation based in Nigeria. She serves on the board, delivery groups and operational panels of several governmental initiatives. Lade has won several awards and has been recognised both nationally and internationally for the works she does to raise awareness of mental health issues in the communities. She is an internationally recognised motivational speaker, mentor and a life coach.

She is also a director of REOPASS, a Family Navigating Organisation supporting families in crisis, and working with victims who have suffered domestic abuse. She is a multiple award winner and international public speaker, she has spoken at various national and international fora influencing policies and changing lives. She is an elected Councilor under the Labour Party in the Royal Royal Borough of Greenwich, in the United Kingdom.

5

DOMESTIC ABUSE IN AFRICA
– A FOCUS ON NIGERIA

Margaret O. Ojo

The National Institute for Health and Care Excellence (NICE) defines domestic violence and abuse as 'any incidents of controlling, coercive or threatening behaviour, violence, or abuse between those aged 16 or over who are or have been intimate partners or family members regardless of gender or sexuality' (NICE, 2016). Domestic abuse includes psychological physical, sexual, financial and emotional abuse as well as honour-based violence and forced marriages. Having a long-term illness or disability, including mental health problems, increases a person's risk of experiencing domestic violence or abuse.

Domestic violence is one of the most significant social problems and greatest human rights violations that we currently face in Nigeria. This problem is not confined to Nigeria; it is also prevalent across Africa and other parts of the world. Unfortunately, domestic violence shows no signs of decreasing in Nigeria due to a cultural belief that it is socially acceptable to hit a woman as a means of disciplining a spouse. Common types of abuse against women in Nigeria include rape, acid-attacks, molestation, wife-beating and corporal punishment. Many of these crimes go unreported—partly because of a lack of sufficient evidence, but more due to the fear of social stigma. The patriarchal nature of Nigerian society is one of the main reasons that domestic abuse against women continues to be prevalent in the country. It is commonly perceived that husbands are justified in using violence against wives as a tool to chastise and improve them.

In sub-Saharan Africa, a woman loses her rights upon marriage; she is expected to be implicitly obedient to her man and forfeit any sense of self and identity. Doing so is widely encouraged and socially accepted. Patriarchal societal structures are dominant amongst the Yoruba, Igbo and Hausa, which has facilitated an almost blind justification of domestic abuse towards women. A woman in these societies is in most cases obligated to give her husband full ownership of herself upon marriage, thereby literarily enabling her objectification and dehumanisation.

DOMESTIC ABUSE AND VIOLENCE TOWARDS WOMEN IN NIGERIA

Abuse and violence towards women in Nigeria and Africa as a whole extend far beyond the occasional beating or manhandling, that they endure. It also includes female genital mutilation, forced marriages, marital and non-marital rape, sexual harassment at work and educational institutions, forced prostitution, forced abortions, trafficking and other harmful practices. Age is not a barrier preventing this type of criminality; for example, a local organisation in Zaria, Nigeria, found that 16% of patients with sexually transmitted diseases (STDs) were under the age of 5, a sign that children are being sexually assaulted and raped. (Africa Renewal, 2007).

In recent years, new forms of violence toward women have emerged in Africa. There have been recent reports in Nigeria of women being brutalised and raped by the police and other local forces. In 2019, a group of women were arrested during a police raid in the Federal Capital, Abuja. They were accused of being sex-workers, and they claimed to have been raped repeatedly by officers upon their arrival to the police station. (BBC News Lagos, 2020).

Reports such as these are increasing all over Nigeria. Police raping women with impunity is now rampant in many states across Nigeria, and such incidents preclude women who are victims of violence and abuse from seeking refuge or even reporting these cases at police stations. Victims are not reassured that they will receive the help they need; even worse, there is the possibility that they may be raped and re-victimised in the process.

Other factors contributing to violence against women in Nigeria include Sharia law, which often discriminates against

Muslim women. Widely practised in the Northern part of Nigeria, the Sharia system of justice puts a lot of women at risk of violence and sometimes death. Issues such as gender inequality and the offence of adultery (*zina*) are among various factors that instigate abuse and violence against women. Some scholars dispute such claims and propose that these acts are not due to the imposition of Sharia law but rather are conceived by a cultural imperative, which falsely attributes such atrocities to religion. Although such debates persist, what is remains undisputed is that these acts are committed against women consistently and with impunity.

Practised in Nigeria and across Africa, female genital mutilation (FGM) entails the partial or complete removal of the external genitalia or other injury to the female genital organs. It is believed among some groups that this act should be performed to make women more marriageable and prevent promiscuity; however, this practice can be very debilitating for women, causing severe bleeding and problems urinating in the short term, and later contributing to the formation of cysts, infections, childbirth complications and an increased risk of new-born mortality. FGM has come to global attention; the World Health Organisation (WHO, 2020) has condemned all forms of FGM and opposes health care providers performing these acts (medicalisation of FGM).

Nigeria is a tough place to seek justice for abuse and violence, especially when the victims are women, and many of these atrocities go unreported and unpunished for this reason. Many women choose not to report cases for fear of stigmatisation, police extortion, a lack of confidence in the judicial system, or—worse still—because the victim may not even recognise the act as being a crime. The latter is case for many women who experience marital rape. Those who are brave enough to report such acts have been met with scorn and sometimes even berated for not performing their marital duties. Other rape victims are sometimes berated for their style of dress, with the insinuation being that the victims supposedly 'asked for it'.

According to the Nigerian Bureau of Statistics, there were 2,279 reported cases of rape and indecent assault, 1164 reported cases of 'unnatural offences' (i.e. anal sex), and 0 convictions in 2017. Only one state (out of 36) reported no cases of indecent assault.

I recently came across a Facebook forum chaired by Sola Adeboye called the Human Rights Defenders and Access to Justice Advocacy Centre. Adeboye has set up a walk-in centre for victims within his locality to report any incidences of abuse, violence or injustices to which they are subjected, and he tries to facilitate some form of advocacy for them to pursue justice. He streams it live on Facebook and always has at least 3,000 people watching at any one time. Initially, I was quite impressed with his initiative; however, I developed some reservations once I had joined him on a few of the cases. I felt that there were some risks related to how he was handling some of the cases; my first concern was that it was a one-man panel.

On one occasion, a woman and her 16-year-old daughter reported that her husband was physically abusing the wife and implied that the daughter had sexually assaulted by him. I was shocked by the chairman's line of questioning; it was obvious he had pre-judged the women before he even had the chance to hear the case. I felt that his line of questioning was biased, condescending and heavily laden with subtle innuendos. The 16-year-old's testimony was ridiculed and dismissed without proper investigation. Not once was the mother asked any questions or permitted to talk. Ultimately, the child and woman were told off and sent on their way with the same man about whom they had come to complain. I was greatly concerned about the child and woman, as nothing was put in place to ensure their safety.

A single person acting as the investigator, jury, and judge, presents the risk that only one point of view is offered in judgement, which empowers a biased and personalised opinion, as whatever he feels is right or wrong becomes the judgement. To offer such advocacy without adequate professional counselling and safeguards in place could present a risk to victims. Having said that, it was quite refreshing to see that Adebayo is at least bringing some awareness of the consequences for violence and domestic abuse to grassroots communities.

DOMESTIC ABUSE AGAINST MEN

While domestic abuse is mostly inflicted on women in Nigeria, there are also cases when men have been victimised. The fact that Nigeria is a patriarchal society that brands women the 'weaker sex' and men the 'head of household' means that men who suffer domestic abuse at the hands of women are either too embarrassed to report it, and those who do will likely be ignored or not believed.

Most writers on domestic abuse highlight it as 'a luxuriating iniquity against Nigerian women' (e.g. Anyogu and Arinze-Umobi, 2011, pg. 152). Hamberger et al (1992) and Saunders (1986) purport that most women who commit domestic abuse on men only do so to defend themselves against attacks perpetrated by men. While it is true that the majority of attacks committed by women against men are likely due to self-defence, one cannot ignore that men have also been exposed to domestic violence and become victims due to other factors. Studies have found that 84% of men have been violated or victimised at least once by a woman, including 59% who have suffered sexual violence, 61% who have endured psychological violence and 76% who have experienced verbal violence (Fakankinnu, 2007).

While I do not doubt the plausibility of the data, I do feel that in current times, there has been a rise in Nigerian women who have killed their men in a jealous rage or for other reasons. For instance, Maryam Sanda allegedly stabbed her husband,

Bilyaminu Bello, the son of a former national chairman of the People's Democratic Party (PDP), on the 18th of November 2017 after she found photos of a nude woman on his phone. Although Sanda claimed that he died from slipping and falling on a broken bottle when she went into a fit of rage and began shouting and threatening him, the forensic examination determined that the fatal wound was in fact caused by a kitchen knife. Initially, Sanda was cleared of the crime, as her mother and brother had cleaned the crime scene prior to officers arriving, and no evidence was found. While this seemed to benefit her cause, during the trial, this was considered tampering with evidence. At her trial, FCT High Court Judge Yusuf Halilu convicted Sanda based on the law of 'doctrine last seen', which puts the burden of proof on the last person to be seen with the deceased. Justice Halilu based his judgment on the evidence before him and irrevocably sentenced her to death by hanging (The Guardian, 2020).

While the Sanda incident could constitute an example of domestic abuse against men, the prevalence of such events is incomparable to the number of cases of violence against women. Notably, the results of a recent Spousal Violence poll by NOIPolls indicated that 56% of surveyed Nigerians perceived that violence against WOMEN by MEN is prevalent and 47% believed the violence against MEN by WOMEN is prevalent. As this is merely a poll reporting on the opinion of Nigerians, it does not give an accurate account of the number of men or women who are victims of domestic abuse. What could be said to be encouraging about the results is that 100% of the survey participants stated that it is not justifiable for either husbands or wives to assault/abuse or kill their spouses (NOIPolls, 2020).

A more accurate reflection of domestic violence prevalence was published in *BMC Women's Health*. A recent cross-sectional study based on the latest Nigerian Demographic Health Survey (2013) examined the effect of individual- and community-level factors on intimate partner violence (IPV) in Nigeria, with a focus on women's status and norms among men. Among 20,802 ever-partnered women aged 15–49, one in four women reported having ever experienced intimate partner violence (Benebo, et al., 2018). This is a very disturbing statistic, and the Nigerian government urgently needs to place measures to intervene and mitigate this issue higher on their list of priorities.

OTHER TYPES OF DOMESTIC ABUSE AND VIOLENCE

Other forms of domestic violence that relate to (intimate partner abuse) IPV are also meted out to women in Nigeria. This section discusses several forms of abuse that are prevalent in our communities but are often ignored and do not get the attention they deserve.

Domestic Violence – Forced Abortions.

A forced abortion occurs when a perpetrator causes an intentional termination of pregnancy without the consent of the victim. In most cases, the victim is taken advantage of when she is in her most weakened state, either by being beaten to submission or coerced with other bullying or gaslighting techniques. In some cases, the perpetrator may cause the abortion by stealthily administering medication or chemicals that induce the loss of the foetus.

While this may not seem obvious, it is commonplace in communities across Nigeria for women to face domestic abuse and violence from their partners for refusing to terminate a pregnancy. For instance, on the 20th of June 2020, it was reported that a husband in Ondo State, Nigeria allegedly beat his wife of two years for refusing to agree to abort her pregnancy. The couple already had one child, and the wife was three months pregnant. She was violently brutalised and sustained bruises all over her body; moreover, it was reported that the husband had inserted his hand into her private parts in an attempt to abort the baby himself. In most cases when these stories are reported, the sectionalisation of the actual incidence is limited to what is captured, and there is no real reference of any measures implemented for the perpetrator to face justice (Pulse.NG, 2020). In this case, family members spoke out to confirm that the couple's relationship had been fraught with domestic abuse issues. As the wife's family stated, 'Our sister had been complaining to us for a long time about how her husband had been maltreating her over every single issue since they got married. We always settle issues for them because there is no perfect marriage but her sin this time around was her refusal to abort her three-month-old pregnancy which she had for him'.

Violence in Nigeria seems to be culturally rooted, and even when the perpetrators of domestic abuse are confronted and brought before the law, there is a lackadaisical approach to meting out justice. In most cases it is believed that it is normal for domestic abuse to occur in marriages. The blame is laid on the woman, and they are coerced to forgive and remain with husbands and partners who routinely abuse them.

Bullying

Although bullying is a subtle form of abuse, it deserves mention because of the immense anxiety and stress that it causes in the victim. Moreover, in most cases, bullying eventually leads to physical abuse. Bullying can manifest in various forms, including verbal, emotional and spiritual abuse. These are very serious types of abuse that often go unrecognised if the victim is exposed to it on a regular basis. Many women assume that they would recognise if they were being verbally abused, as they perceive it as being characterised by yelling, and name calling, and other more obvious forms of disparagement.

Bullying can have longer term effects on victims than physical wounds. Bullying tends to have negative impacts on victims' emotional and psychological state and could lead to poor mental health. The effects of bullying may be difficult to detect, as there are no tell-tale signs such as bruises or other physical wounds. Some common signs of bullying include suicide attempts, difficulty sleeping and having frequent nightmares, changes in eating habits, loss of interest in work, self-harm and lowered self-esteem.

Gaslighting

Gaslighting is a term that was coined from a 1938 play by Patrick Hamilton, known as 'Angel Street', which was later developed into the film 'Gas Light' directed by Alfred Hitchcock (Thomas, 2018). The movie is about a husband who abuses, controls, and cuts his wife off from her friends and family and tries to make her feel like she is going insane by making subtle changes to her environment. His efforts go as far as steadily dimming the flame on the gas lamp (Thomas, 2018).Due to the accuracy of the film's portrayal of the husband's controlling and toxic actions and their repercussions, psychologists and counsellors began to use the term 'gaslighting' to label this type of emotionally abusive behaviour.

Gaslighting features prominently in marriage and dating relationships; however, it can also occur in friendships and amongst family members. The perpetrator is very manipulative and controlling, and they may use combination of verbal abuse tactics. It is a very subtle, cunning and covert type of emotional abuse whereby the bully or abuser makes the victim question their judgement and understanding of reality (Breines, 2012). A person being gaslighted will frequently question their perception of reality and doubt their perceptions and even their memories. The victim is left confused and will often question whether they are sane. Some characteristics of a gaslighter include:

♦ **Pathological lying** – A gaslighter will blatantly lie to their victim's face and will never back down or change their opinion. A gaslighter has the power and conviction to make their victim begin believing their lies; this is one of the most powerful weapons they have in their arsenal.

♦ **Rumour spreading and perpetual gossiping** - While they appear sympathetic and empathetic to their victim's needs or situations, behind their backs, gaslighters subtly spread deadly rumours informing on their victim's lack of stability and sanity. This is a very effective tool, as the perpetrator is believed in most cases. The gaslighter will also lie and inform the victim that other friends or family think that they are insane.

♦ **Never accepting blame or responsibility** – If a gaslighter is faced with an accusation, they either change the subject or blatantly lie. A gaslighter will accuse the victim of making things up and implying that what they are being accused of simply did not happen, thereby creating further confusion and self-doubt. This behaviour can make the victim feel frustrated, as there is no acknowledgement of the pain they feel, and they are left in a position where they are unable to move on or heal.

'When you deal with someone who never acknowledges your thoughts, your feelings, or your beliefs, you will begin to question them yourself. What's more, you never feel validated or understood, which can be extremely difficult to cope with' (Verywellmind, 2021).

♦ **Blame shifting** – Another effective tool in the gas lighter's arsenal is to twist the victim's discussions to affix blame on them. The gaslighter manipulates the situation such that the victim ultimately believes they are the cause of the perpetrator's bad behaviour.

♦ **Use of compassionate words** – The perpetrator usually resorts to using kind and loving words to smooth over a situation. These words do not express the gas lighter's true feelings but rather are what they know that the victim would like to hear. Compassionate words are used to reel in the victim for the moment; however, the perpetrator never changes their behaviour but rather repeatedly uses this tactic.

'When you are dealing with someone who uses gaslighting as a manipulation tool, pay close attention to their actions, not their words. Is this person truly loving or are they only saying loving things?' (Verywellmind, 2021).

Twisting and reframing conversations – This is a tactic that a gaslighter will use when discussing past events. For instance, the perpetrator will twist an incident of physical abuse in their own favour, which may cause the victim to doubt their memory of what actually happened.

The gaslighter is one of the worst perpetrators of domestic abuse. Their behaviour can cause anxiety, depression, low-mood, panic attacks and nervous breakdowns. Victims should look for the signs below and seek help immediately if they recognise any of them. (Verywellmind, 2021).

♦ Doubting your feelings of reality.

♦ Questioning your judgement and perceptions.

♦ Feeling of vulnerability and insecurity.

♦ Feeling alone and powerless.

♦ Wondering if you are stupid and crazy.

♦ Feeling disappointed in yourself.

- Feeling confused.

- Worrying that you are too sensitive.

- Having a sense of impending doom.

- Spending a lot of time apologising.

- Feeling inadequate.

- Second-guessing yourself.

- Assuming others are disappointed in you.

- Wondering what is wrong with you.

- Struggling to make decisions.

If you believe that your partner or anyone else with whom you are in a relationship is enabling any of the above symptoms, immediately seek professional help or speak to someone. It is imperative to understand that you are not the one at fault. The person that who has decided to inflict this on you is exhibiting predatory behaviour and they are the one responsible for their actions, not you!

CHALLENGES

There are numerous cultural, social, traditional and economic factors that hinder efforts to tackle domestic abuse in Nigeria. As mentioned above, the patriarchal social structure poses an enormous obstacle, as the needs of the man are upheld over those of the woman. The average woman in Nigeria does not have an independent voice and has been systematically robbed of her sense of worth and value due to decades of imbalances in power and control within the home and the broader society. Over the years, women have accepted their role as subservient partners and readily relinquish their power to their husbands or partners, as they believe it is culturally and traditionally expected.

To the average Nigerian woman, the concept of marriage evokes a sense of gratitude that plays to the sentiment of it being a 'favour' conferred upon them rather than a union of two people as partners in a personal relationship. There is a set of values that is expected of the wife-to-be, and failure to meet them could lead to severe repercussions such as domestic abuse, violence, or divorce. The notion that an unmarried woman is of no consequential value or worth facilitates an almost unnatural clamour for women to seek an available man to marry in order to avoid the stigma of being classified as unmarried. Once a woman has attained the title of 'being married', the next hurdle they face is to keep the marriage at all costs—in some cases, even at the cost of their lives or those of their children.

Social media has provided an eye opener to what the Nigerian woman of today understands, expects, and is willing to accept in the name of marriage. It is sometimes alarming to see how many women still believe that it is a husband's right to chastise his wife using various forms of domestic abuse and violence, even rape. I was recently engaged on a social media thread that featured a young Nigerian woman who had been raped by her partner. Almost all of the women who responded were critical of her being so emotional about the incident, and some were asking what the problem was. From their perspective, after all, she had had sex with him before, and it was only sex anyway! Some stated that she should be thankful it was not a stranger. I received a great deal of reproach when I responded that in fact, 'it would have been better if it were a stranger'. In my opinion, the conversation evinced a lack of understanding of the meaning of trust and love in a relationship and highlighted that many Nigerian women view themselves as objects to be used and abused. Sadly, some even think that such treatment is deserved. This type of rhetoric further furnishes men with power and diminishes the respect of the women who have committed themselves to be in a relationship with them.

During my interactions on social media, I discovered that a lot of women in Nigeria, consider rape to be merely a sex act and diminish the negative physical and psychological impacts. I was forced to further clarify the issue by describing an incident of rape that involved the use of an object rather than the man's sexual organ, which resulted in damage to the victim's internal organs and haemorrhaging that ultimately led to her death. Education is needed to highlight the real impacts of rape and engender a deeper understanding of the value and rights we have as women in the face of this type of violation.

A pan-African online publication for attorneys recently observed that the Nigerian Constitution prohibits foreign husbands of Nigerian women from attaining Nigerian citizenship. Another section of the Nigerian penal code that is applicable in Northern Nigeria allows spousal battery as a form of chastising a wife so long as grievous harm does not result. There is also a provision in the Labour Act that prohibits women from working at night. Such measures highlight how the patriarchal regime has impacted laws affecting Nigerian women. Women's rights activists and others advocates should clamour for such laws to be reviewed and abolished.

CONCLUSION

Although domestic abuse and violence are still rampant in the Nigerian society, there have been some efforts towards addressing these issues. In 2006, Nigeria adopted a Framework and Plan of Action for the National Gender Policy, and the federal and state governments adopted several legislative and policy instruments, including The Violence Against Persons Prohibition Act of 2015, which outlawed female genital mutilation, harmful widowhood and traditional practices, and all forms of violence against persons in both private and public life (United Nations, Africa Renewal, n.d.).

Some independent states such as Ekiti and Lagos state are passing laws such as the Law on Gender-Based Violence, which in addition to domestic violence also prohibits economic abuse resulting in a woman's inability to access funds or provide food, shelter, and basic needs. The Ekiti state government also provided a fund to address some of these economic needs and reduce the occurrence of domestic abuse stemming from them.

There is now an action line for victims of domestic abuse to call, the DSVRT (Lagos State Domestic Sexual and Violence Response Team). As the website states, 'DSVRT is a collection of professional service providers and officials that respond as a group and in a timely fashion to the various needs of domestic and sexual violence survivors by providing legal, medical, emergency assistance, counselling, and psychological and psychosocial support'. The line can be contacted toll free at (+234) 8000333333 or by texting 'HELP' to 6820 or dialling *6820#.

Although some contingencies are beginning to emerge to combat this problem in Nigeria, much more needs to be done, and it must be done more quickly. Education about domestic abuse and violence should be included in the national curriculum. The government needs to recognise this as a national problem and actively fund and promote region-wide preventative initiatives. Tougher laws must be enacted, and there should be stronger enforcement in cases of violence against women. Perpetrators should face legal actions and be punished for their crimes. A better support network is required for victims of domestic abuse, and the government should fund NGOs for this cause. Targeted training should be provided to healthcare professionals on how to identify and intervene in domestic abuse issues impacting men and women, and local authorities and government agencies should collaborate to conduct such programs. The Nigerian police force's training should include mandatory courses that inform them about domestic abuse and violence against women and provide a framework for intervention. Overall, a nationwide enlightenment is required, and there should be campaigns for women's rights in Nigeria, especially those that educate about domestic abuse and violence.

REFERENCES

Africa Renewal, 2007. *Taking on violence against women in Africa.* [Online] Available at: https://www.un.org/africarenewal/magazine/july-2007/taking-violence-against-women-africa [Accessed 12 February 2021].

Aloy, o., Jorge, N. & Nnamdi, O., 2019. Domestic Violence Victimisation in Nigeria: The Often Ignored Perspective. *International Journal for International Feminist Studies,* November, 5(1-2), p. 12.

BBC News Lagos, 2020. *#WeAreTired: Nigerian women speak out over wave of violence.* [Online] Available at: https://www.bbc.co.uk/news/world-africa-52889965 [Accessed 13 February 2021].

BBC NEWS Pidgin, 2020. *Maryam Sanda: 'Why cases of women wey dey kill dia husband still fit rise'.* [Online] Available at: https://www.bbc.com/pidgin/tori-51280918 [Accessed 10 February 2021].

Benebo, F., Schumann, B. & Vaezghasemi, M., 2018. Intimate partner violence against women in Nigeria: a multilevel study investigating the effect of women's status and community norms. *BMC Women's Health*, 29 August, p. 18.

Breines, J., 2012. Call me crazy: The subtle power of gaslighting. *Berkeley Science Review.*

Danielle, P., 2020. *Washington Post - Africa - She was found guilty of killing her husband. Her punishment: hanging.* [Online] Available at: https://www.washingtonpost.com/world/she-was-found-guilty-of-killing-her-husband-her-punishment-hanging/2020/01/29/9a61db18-4296-11ea-abff-5ab1ba98b405_story.html [Accessed 12 February 2021].

Krug, E. G. et al., 2002. *World Health Organisation - World report on violence and health,* Geneva: World Health Organisation.

NICE, 2016. *Domestic violence and abuse - Quality standards [QS 116].* [Online] Available at: https://www.nice.org.uk/guidance/qs116 [Accessed 2 February 2021].

NOIPolls, 2020. *Spousal violence poll result.* [Online] Available at: https://noi-polls.com/spousal-violence-poll-result/ [Accessed 12 February 2021].

Pulse.NG, 2020. *Man beats up wife, inserts hand in her genital to abort 3-month-old pregnancy.* [Online] Available at: https://www.pulse.ng/news/metro/man-beats-up-wife-inserts-hand-in-her-genital-to-abort-3-month-old-pregnancy/ps4mftn [Accessed 14 February 2021].

Thomas, L., 2018. Gaslight and Gaslighting. *The Lancet Psychiatry,* 5 (2), pp. 117-118.

United Nations, Africa Renewal, n.d. *16 Days of Activism - Nigerian women say 'no' to gender-based violence.* [Online] Available at: https://www.un.org/africarenewal/news/nigerian-women-say-%E2%80%98no%E2%80%99-gender-based-violence [Accessed 1 February 2021].

Verywellmind, 2021. *What is Gaslighting.* [Online] Available at: https://www.verywellmind.com/is-someone-gaslighting-you-4147470 [Accessed 14 February 2021].

World Health Organisation, 2013. *Global and regional estimates of violence against women Prevalence and health effects of intimate partner violence and non-partner sexual violence.* [Online] Available at: http://www.who.int/reproductivehealth/publications/violence/9789241564625/en/ [Accessed 10 February 2021].

World Health Organisation, 2020. *Female Genital Mutilation.* [Online] Available at: https://www.who.int/news-room/fact-sheets/detail/female-genital-mutilation#:~:text=Female%20genital%20mutilation%20(FGM)%20involves,benefits%20for%20girls%20and%20women. [Accessed 14 February 2021].

BIOGRAPHY

Margaret Ojo

Margaret Ojo is a Project Manager by day, a private Chef on the weekends and a Crypto currency enthusiast all the time. Margaret is also a content writer and avid reader. Born in the UK she lived her formative years from 6-19 years of age in her home country Nigeria until she returned back to the UK.

Margaret stated that living in Nigeria from the age of 6 till 19 exposed her to the trauma a lot of Nigerian women went through in terms of various forms of domestic abuse. Margaret states that she remained thankful to her parents that did not sign up to the extreme types of abuse she saw other children and women go through. Having witnessed some girls go through female genital mutilation (FGM), and other extreme forms of spousal abuse and violence, she was moved and vowed to advocate for victims of these abuses. Margaret reports that now that she resides in the UK, she was encouraged to research, write and highlight the impact of these crimes against women and how the African socio-cultural values play a role in influencing this.

PART 2

Essays on
Migration Drivers

6

TRENDS IN

AFRICAN MIGRATION

Olivia Bola J-Olajide Aluko

Stories abound of African migrants drowning in the Mediterranean or suffocating on board trucks in their desperate efforts to arrive in the UK or other parts of Europe. Coupled with images of impoverished African children shown on television, such images create the impression that the continent has collapsed, and that millions of Africans are trying to escape the continent. As a consequence, those migrants and refugees who eventually make their way to the UK are often treated with scorn and dismissed as scavengers. In fact, various degrading terms have been used to describe immigrants from Africa, such as 'hordes' 'swarms' and even 'cockroaches'. There is no doubt that the Libyan migration and slave trade crises have only added fuel to such perceptions.

Forced migration occurs when a person is moved against their will, such as during the Trans-Atlantic Slave Trade or in the present time through human trafficking in various forms and modern slavery, as seen in the Libyan slave trade crisis. Some moves are triggered by external factors, such as natural disasters or civil wars, whereby the victims become displaced and are forced to seek refuge elsewhere. These people are described as 'refugees' or 'asylum seekers' (Weinstein & Pillai, 2001). The UK follows the Geneva Convention on refugees in defining a refugee as someone who has fled their own country because of a 'well-founded fear of being persecuted for reasons of race, religion, nationality, membership of a particular social group or political opinion' (UNHCR, 2011). Similarly, the United Nations High Commission for Refugees (UNHCR) defines refugees as:

> Individuals recognized under the 1951 Convention relating to the Status of Refugees, its 1967 Protocol, the 1969 OAU Convention Governing the Specific Aspects of Refugee Problems in Africa, those recognized in accordance with the UNHCR Statute, individuals granted complementary forms of protection, and those enjoying temporary protection (UNHCR, 1992).

The British government also allows people to remain in the country without granting them refugee status. An asylum seeker is someone who has applied to the Home Office for refugee status or one of those other forms of international protection, and is awaiting a decision on that application. In 2016, nearly 90% of the 39,000 asylum seekers in the UK travelled from Asian or African countries, with the top five nationalities being Iranian, Pakistani, Iraqi, Afghan and Bangladeshi, yet Syrians received the most asylum grants without an appeal being needed, followed by Iranians, Eritreans, Sudanese and Afghans (McKinney, 2016).

While the recent migrant crisis has drawn the world's attention to African refugees, Africa in fact has a long history of both internal and international migration, with millions of individuals moving both within and beyond the continent since colonialism. As seen in Table 2 and Figure 2 below, according to the World Bank, between 1980 and 2010, the number of Africans migrating from their countries of origin has doubled to about 30.6 million (Ehrhart, Le Goff, Rocher, & Singh, 2014). In other words, about 3% of the country's population are scattered in different countries and continents all over the world.

It is not clear how many African migrants have left Africa since 2010; however, a 2013 United Nations Department of Economic and Social Affairs (UN DESA) report indicated that about 11.3 million people from the continent were living in developed countries in Europe, North America and elsewhere (UN DESA Population Division, 2013). This number does not take into consideration those who have left Africa for these countries through illegal means. In 2015, the UN DESA Population Division (2015) estimated that 14% of international migrants in the world originated from Africa. Yet, African migration rates are actually currently among the lowest in the world, only higher than those of Asia and North America (Shimeles, 2018). Moreover, contrary to media hype about African migration swamping the Western countries, half of these African migrants move to other countries within Africa.

The factors that trigger migration and keep it going once begun are described as the 'drivers of migration' (Massey et al., 1998). As noted above, the personal characteristics of migrants inform their decisions. Multiple factors have been linked to the migration of Africans, such as 'human security,' environmental factors, and a host of other social and economic issue. The lack of political freedom or civil liberties and endemic corruption are some of the reasons that migrants leave Africa. Conflicts and ongoing wars like some parts of South Sudan, Somalia, and the Democratic Republic of Congo make the people in these countries vulnerable, and many people have had to flee due to fear for their lives. Corruption has had a significant role in driving migrants from their countries of origin, particularly those who speak out against corrupt leadership or become whistle-blowers in exposing corrupt practices. Yet, overall, current patterns of Black African migrations to the UK are different from those of the pre-colonial period, when such movements were primarily involuntary. Migration trends of Black Africans in the 21st century tend to be more choice-driven in nature, whereby economic factors are the main drivers of moves to developed countries. Despite independence from colonial rule, Africa has not been able to achieve the kind of educational and economic development that would sustain job opportunities for its growing population. Because of this, its people have often emigrated out of the continent to search for job opportunities elsewhere with some risking their lives in the process. Many professionals and students migrate to Western countries. The impact of the migrants who have left Africa is especially noticeable in the health sector, resulting in a brain drain from Africa and a brain gain in the developed world.

One of the determinants of migration is cost, including travel and relocation, which is likely why migrants from richer African countries tend to migrate to destinations outside of Africa. The poorer the country, the less affordable it becomes to travel far in search of better opportunities. While migrants from wealthier origin countries tend to be better educated and skilled, migration has served as a lifeline for many poorer African countries through the flow of remittances. In most cases for Africans, migration is not only a singular decision, but it also transcends households, and it creates responsibilities. Remittances provide consumption smoothing for poor families, and serve as a source of investment at the household level for education, assets, and other amenities. For example, a male migrant may move to the UK, but he will often leave behind his wife and children or siblings for whom he owes responsibilities. Until he can bring these family members over to the country of destination, he may have to send remittances for their upkeep. Remittances serve as an important factor in reducing asset inequality in Africa (Shimeles & Nabasaga, forthcoming). For many African countries, the reliable funds from remissions have become the most important source of foreign exchange.

Table 2. Estimated total stocks of migration from, to, and within Africa, 1960-2000 (Flahaux & De Haas, 2016).

Year	From Africa to the rest of the world	From the rest of the world to Africa
1960	1,830776	2,811930
1980	5,418096	1,872502
2000	8,734478	1,532746

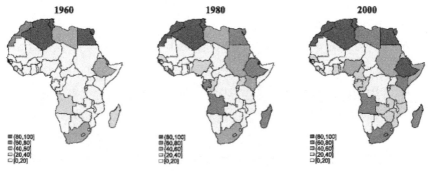

Figure 2. Emigration intensity from African countries, 1960-2000 (emigrants per 1000 people born in each country). Note. Reprinted from 'African migration: trends, patterns, drivers,' by M-L. Flahaus and H. De Haas, 2016. Comparative Migration Studies, 4, 1. Retrieved fromhttps://doi.org/10.1186/s40878-015-0015-6 Copyright 2016, M-L. Flahaus and H. De Haas.

INTERNAL MIGRATION

Internal migration refers to a change of residence within national boundaries, such as between states, provinces, cities, or municipalities. Internal migration is a common feature in Africa and takes place on a larger scale than international migration, even though this is rarely stated. To appreciate migration determinants within Africa, it is important to understand the continent's historical evolution. The phenomenon of internal migration in Africa can be better understood within the context of political and historical evolution of African societies. The effects of colonisation and decolonisation on the economy and indirectly on migration are most visible when examined in the context of the pre-colonial, the colonial and post-colonial era. Prior to colonisation, movement from one place to another within Africa was largely free and had much less restrictions than exist now. In the pre-colonial era, population movements in Africa were largely associated with the prevailing socio-political and ecological conditions, especially internecine warfare, natural disasters and the search for farmland or new territories to settle. Such movements were unstructured, occurred in groups, and the migrants were demographically undifferentiated (Adepoju, 1979). By the 1960s, however, the newly independent nation-states had begun to set up regulations governing immigration, and during the 1960s-1980s, decolonisation and antagonism between recently created states is credited with increasing barriers to movement within the continent. Generally, most areas have remained relatively closed to migrants, though West and Southern Africa remain relatively open. Yet, as shown in Figures 3–6, except for North Africa, throughout the continent, most migrant movements occur within the continent, particularly between neighbouring countries, partly reflecting the relatively more flexible migration policies adopted by African countries over the years. Smaller populations and surface account for the high migration levels in many West-African countries (Flahaux & De Haas, 2016). Additionally, West African countries are made up of many ethnic groups, many of which cross borders, and established strong network connections across neighbouring countries, which have endured since colonial rule. West African countries also enjoy a visa-free movement between ECOWAS (Economic Community of West African States) countries. Interestingly, Southern Africa is the only region in the continent that has become more open to internal migration, particularly since the collapse of the restrictive apartheid regime in South Africa (Flahaux & De Haas, 2016). Currently, African countries host more than 26% of the world's refugee population (UNHCR, 2001-2017).

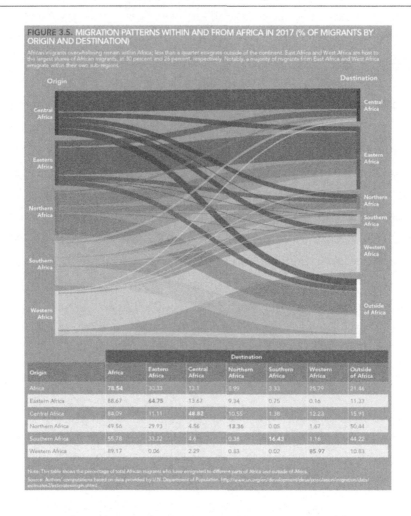

Figure 3. African Migration Patterns, 2017. Reprinted from 'Understanding the patterns and causes of African migration: Some facts,' by A. Shimeles, 2018. In B.S. Coulibaly (ed.), Foresight Africa: Top priorities for the Continent in 2018 (pp. 54-57). Washington, D.C.: The Brookings Institution. Retrieved from https://www.brookings.edu/wp-content/uploads/2018/01/foresight-2018_full_web_final1.pdf

Figure 4. Refugee population by origin in SSA, 1990-2013

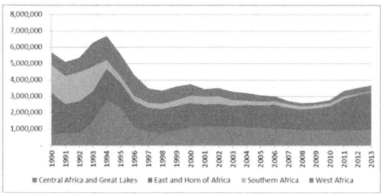

Note: Authors' aggregation based on UNHCR statistical population online dataset, accessed in September 2014.

7

Figure 4. African refugee populations, 1990-2013.

Reprinted from 'Forced displacement and refugees in Sub-Saharan Africa: An economic inquiry,' by P. Verwimp and J-F. Maystadt, 2015. Policy Research Working Paper 7517. Washington, DC: The World Bank group (https://openknowledge.worldbank.org/bitstream/handle/10986/23481/Forced0displac00an0economic0inquiry.pdf?sequence=1). Copyright 2015, The World Bank Group.

Top 10 by asylum, based on 2013				
	1990	2000	2010	2013
Kenya	14,249	206,106	402,905	534,938
Chad		17,692	347,939	434,479
Ethiopia	773,764	197,959	154,295	433,936
Uganda	145,718	236,622	135,801	220,555
Sudan*	1,031,050	414,928	178,308	159,857
Cameroon	49,876	43,680	104,275	114,753
Dem. Rep. of the Congo	416,435	332,509	166,336	113,362
United Rep. of Tanzania	265,184	680,862	109,286	102,099
Mauritania	60,000	350	26,717	92,767
Rwanda	23,601	28,398	55,398	73,349

Figure 5. Top ten African countries receiving refugees, 2010.

Reprinted from 'Forced displacement and refugees in Sub-Saharan Africa: An economic inquiry,' by P. Verwimp and J-F. Maystadt, 2015. Policy Research Working Paper 7517. Washington, DC: The World Bank group (https://openknowledge.worldbank.org/bitstream/handle/10986/23481/Forced0displac00an0economic0inquiry.pdf?sequence=1). Copyright 2015, the World Bank Group.

Table 3. Weighted ranking of host countries in SSA (top 20 in SSA)

Number of refugees, 2013		Refugees to 1,000 inhabitants		Refugees to 1,000 km²	
Kenya	534,938	Chad	33.88	Rwanda	2,897.11
Chad	434,479	Djibouti	22.93	Burundi	1,680.58
Ethiopia	433,936	South Sudan	20.32	Djibouti	919.76
South Sudan	229,587	Liberia	12.40	Kenya	914.79
Uganda	220,555	Kenya	12.06	Uganda	910.04
Sudan	159,857	Congo, Rep. of	11.47	Gambia	882.36
Cameroon	114,753	Rwanda	6.23	Liberia	553.04
Dem. Rep. of the Congo	113,362	Uganda	5.87	Ethiopia	383.53
United Rep. of Tanzania	102,099	Gambia	5.17	Togo	359.88
Rwanda	73,349	Cameroon	5.16	South Sudan	355.23
South Africa	65,881	Guinea-Bissau	5.01	Chad	340.92
Niger	57,661	Ethiopia	4.61	Guinea-Bissau	250.24
Liberia	53,253	Burundi	4.48	Cameroon	245.04
Congo	51,037	Sudan	4.21	Congo, Rep. of	148.69
Burundi	45,490	Niger	3.23	United Rep. of Tanzania	107.95
Burkina Faso	29,234	Central African Rep.	3.10	Burkina Faso	106.02
Angola	23,783	Togo	3.02	Sudan	84.76
Zambia	23,594	United Rep. of Tanzania	2.07	Ghana	77.91
Togo	20,613	Burkina Faso	1.73	Senegal	72.14
Djibouti	20,015	Dem. Rep. of the Congo	1.68	South Africa	53.91

Figure 6. Ranking of African countries based on refugee hosting. Reprinted from 'Forced displacement and refugees in Sub-Saharan Africa: An economic inquiry,' by P. Verwimp and J-F. Maystadt, 2015. Policy Research Working Paper 7517. Washington, DC: The World Bank group (https://openknowledge.worldbank.org/bitstream/handle/10986/23481/Forced0displac00an0economic0inquiry.pdf?sequence=1). Copyright 2015, The World Bank Group.

As Figure 7 shows, African refugees seem to have mainly remained on that continent. While many members of the international community are slamming their doors on migrants and refugees from Africa, Syria, Iraq and elsewhere, other African countries are absorbing them. According to the United Nations, developing countries mostly in Africa are taking in a disproportionate number of refugees—currently 80% of the world's refugee population. (Momodu. 2016-2017). These refugees place enormous pressure on water and health care systems in the host countries. Additionally, a special category of refugees in Africa are known as 'internally displaced persons'. Internally displaced people are defined by the UN as:

> persons or groups of persons who have been forced or obliged to flee or to leave their homes or places of habitual residence, in particular as a result of, or in order to avoid the effects of armed conflict, situations of generalised violence, violations of human rights or natural or human-made disasters, and who have not crossed an internationally recognised state border (UNHCR 1992).

Figure 5. Share of refugees hosted in camps, 2013

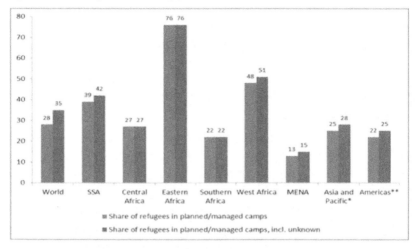

Source: Authors' presentation based on UNHCR Global Trends 2013 (UNHCR 2014).

Figure 7. Regional share of refugees, 2013.

Note. This ranking may be a bit distorted, since refugees are more likely to flee to neighbouring countries.

Other migrations may occur within the country or origin. Many such cases involve individuals who move from rural areas to urban centres, which is often a matter of pride and opportunity for those who move to improve their quality of life and education. Using Nigeria as a common example, it is not uncommon for people to go to villages to pick up young girls around ages of 12-14 to serve as housemaids, who do domestic work in exchange for schooling in the city. People may move from one part of the country to the other to expand their trade. For example, in the 19th century, many Hausas and Fulanis from the Northern part of Nigeria settled in Ibadan, Oyo State of Nigeria, where they became prosperous traders, and such phenomena have continued into the present. Many Africans have migrated in this manner in search of economic opportunity, interacting with members of their host societies and carving out lives for themselves away from their hometown.

INTERNATIONAL MIGRATION

Migrants and refugees fleeing poverty or violent conflict or seeking to improve their quality of life have often used the routes through Libya as a gateway to escape formal border controls to escape to Europe. Over the last four years, about 150,000 migrants and refugees have annually crossed into Europe from Libya in hopes of making their way to a new life (Tharoor, 2017). Within this period, over 3,000 people are reported to have drowned in the Mediterranean Sea, while other migrants became stuck in Libya and unable to leave the country because they became victims of slave trade. In this situation, people have been held against their will, beaten and auctioned into slavery by their captors, with many girls and women raped and often sold into prostitution (Elbagir, Razek, Platt & Jones, 2017). The Libyan slave trade crisis received media and international attention when the scale of abuses finally became publicised. It was estimated that about 400,000 and 1 million migrants have been trapped in Libya, where they have been abused by smugglers and others who have preyed upon their vulnerability and subjected them to excruciating human conditions (Donnelly, 2017).

Whereas internal migration, in principle, implies movement of people within a geographically defined territory unrestricted by legal constraints, an international migrant is invariably confronted with a series of sometimes complex regulations relating to their exit from the country of origin as well as entry into, residence within, and exit from the receiving country. Image plays a major role in the way that refugees are treated, especially in international cases. Although many migrants are fleeing dangerous situations at home, modern migrations are primarily migrations of labour, not of peoples, and they involve migrants taking their place in an organised and structured host society that is oriented towards its citizens (Amin, 1995). There, they generally acquire an inferior status than they would have merited in their country of origin, such as a physician whose license is unrecognised and who must now earn wages driving a taxicab. Refugees are often treated like 'never do wells' in many developed countries, with little consideration given to the valuable roles they often play in the economy. Nonetheless, this does not deter many people from choosing to leave their home societies in search of better opportunities elsewhere.

TRENDS IN WOMEN'S INTERNATIONAL MIGRATION

The migration of women has always been an important component of international movements of people. The Population Division of the UN Department of Economic and Social Affairs (UN DESA 2017) estimated that women and girls comprised 48% of all international migrants in 2017, and their numbers reached as high as 52% in more developed regions. Among destinations, except for Africa and Asia, the numbers of female migrants have slightly exceeded that of males (UN DESA, Population Division, 2017). Among regions of origin, the share of women increased two percent from 2005 to comprise 48.3% of all African migrants, whereas the share of women migrants from upper-middle income countries has declined 43.2–49.1% from 2000 to 2017.

As is the case for men, women's migration outcomes vary depending on both the drivers of their movement and the legality of their positions as immigrants in the receiving country (UN DESA, Division for the Advancement of Women, 2004). Although many women migrate as dependent family members of other migrants or to marry someone in another country, female migrants have also increasingly become a part of international flows of migrant workers (UN DESA, Division for the Advancement of Women, 2004). Most migrant women move voluntarily; however, women and girls have also been forced to leave their countries due to conflict, persecution, environmental degradation, natural disasters or other severe situations impacting their security. For example, women comprise well upwards of 50% of all international migrants in parts of Africa besieged by conflict, such as Democratic Republic of the Congo (UN DESA, Population Division, 2017). In South Sudan, gender-based violence (GBV) is one of the most critical threats to the protection and wellbeing of women and children, and it often leads to their displacement as refugee migrants (UNICEF South Sudan Country Office, 2018). It is not uncommon to read or hear reports of violent acts committed against girls and women in African media. From kidnapping, rape, incest, to the spurious attacks of terror unleashed by Boko Haram, Al Shabaab, the stories are endless. For example, the few women that escaped from the camp of the Boko Haram have narrated the various forms of cruelty that they experienced in the hands of the insurgents, and it is clearly evident that these women had been brainwashed, demeaned and need to be rehabilitated in order to readjust to civil society.

Gender is a critical element of any discussion of the causes and consequences of international migration, including mechanisms leading to migration and decision-making processes concerning this phenomenon. Until recently, approaches to documenting and understanding international migration have generally ignored the participation of women and girls or assumed that the drivers and impacts were identical to those for male migrants (UN DESA, Division for the Advancement of Women, 2004). However, patriarchal social dynamics and resulting gender inequality have had a massive impact on migration experiences of both males and females. In some places, such as Northern Africa, where women comprise only 41.3% of migrants (Gonzales, 2015), the lower share of female migrants is often attributable to their lesser decision-making powers and freedoms, reduced access to resources, and fewer opportunities for independent movement (Ferrant & Tuccio, 2015). Despite some progress, most women in Africa continue to lag behind men in economic development due to patriarchal structures that hinder their participation in the labour market. Some societies still propagate the idea that women are inferior to men, and many women are treated as property and are beaten like children by their husbands. In some African countries, women have no rights, and even in the face of domestic abuse, they cannot rely on the law to protect them. As a consequence of this, many women suffer in silence in the face of ill treatment by their husbands, fathers, or other male relatives.

The incorporation of a gender perspective into migration analyses demands a consideration of female experiences, including relationships and status impact both their ability to engage in international migration and process of migration and settlement in a new country (UN DESA, Division for the Advancement of Women, 2004). In addition, it is important to question how gender systems in destination societies affect the experiences of both male and female migrants. Gender inequality can be a powerful driver of migration when women have economic, political, and social hopes or expectations that will not be realised so long as they remain in the society of origin (UN DESA, Division for the Advancement of Women, 2004). At the social level, issues such as domestic violence, female genital mutilation, honour killings, child marriage and other traditions that repress the freedom of women are a major push factor in migration for many African women. As noted in the introduction to this volume, many Western societies attract women migrants due to a lesser official tolerance for the subjugation of women, such as that which abounds in many African states, and they often seek such countries as destinations when fleeing domestic violence or other heinous acts, such as female genital mutilation or forced marriage, or in search of expanded educational and economic opportunities for themselves and their children. Such factors raise the question of the relative benefits and disadvantages of migration for males and females, as well as how to develop policies and related measures to ensure equal opportunities and outcomes for migrant women and migrant men (UN DESA, Division for the Advancement of Women, 2004).

Grieco and Boyd (1998) identified three broad scales of factors that impact women's migration: 1) individual factors such as age, marital status, role and position in the family, educational status and employment experience; 2) family factors encompassing family size, structure, and socio-economic status; and 3) societal factors such as behavioural norms and cultural values.

Political, social, and economic practices and policies have a gendered impact, and when they discriminate against women, their capacity to fully participate in and contribute to their society is hindered (UN DESA, Division for the Advancement of Women, 2004). Although such limitations often act as drivers of migration, they also impact women's potential of women to migrate and shape the means by which they do so, i.e. whether they can migrate on their own or whether they must be accompanied, or whether they can migrate as a means to increase their own wage-earning capacity or educational level or must do so as wives of migrants or promised wives of men in the destination country. Women's capacity to migrate is also impacted by the presence or absence of social networks in the destination country, as such networks provide valuable information and resources to both make the move possible and facilitate their settlement (UN DESA, Division for the Advancement of Women, 2004).

Women's occupations in their countries of origin are shaped by gender norms that limit their ability to develop certain skills or obtain particular forms or levels of education, and those who migrate for purposes of work are often restricted by their lack of advanced education as well as gender-specific labour demands in the destination countries, such as child care, domestic work, garment manufacturing, or nursing. Such labour norms can limit women's income-generating capacity and make them dependent on employers for fair or decent wages. In some cases, women's migration might be favoured if families consider them to be more likely to be able to take advantage of particular economic opportunities or remit consistently (UN DESA, Division for the Advancement of Women, 2004).

At the family level, men's migration also affects women in countries of origin. In some cases, the departure of male relatives might further restrict women's movements if they are obliged to stay in the homes of other men; however, women remaining behind when their male relatives migrate often undertake income generating activities to compensate for the income lost by the departure of their male relatives, particularly if the men do not regularly send remittances (UN DESA, Division for the Advancement of Women, 2004). Such responsibilities can provide women with greater autonomy and decision-making capacities.

Gender relations and hierarchies and associated policies or practices in destination countries impact migrant women, as well as their legal status and social attitudes towards migrants (UN DESA, Division for the Advancement of Women, 2004). Migrant women whose status is not legal or who are recruited as domestic workers often have little-to-no protections or options in case of abuse. Women who have been trafficked are particularly vulnerable, as they lack social networks and their work is often criminalised. Migrant women are also affected by gender inequality in the society of destination, which can impact issues such as earning capacity as well as legal protections in existing labour laws against exploitation and abuse. At the family level, when male migrants start businesses, female family members such as wives and daughters might be required to work without pay in response to norms established in the country of origin (UN DESA, Division for the Advancement of Women, 2004). However, migrant women who work outside of family businesses can gain financial independence and autonomy within their households (UN DESA, Division for the Advancement of Women, 2004). In such cases, their economic power within the family often gives them leverage to push for different gender relations at home.

Migrant women contribute the economic development of their countries of destination through their competencies and skills, and to their families' well-being and the economic growth of their countries of origin through their remittances (UN DESA, Division for the Advancement of Women, 2004). Those who return home also contribute increased experience and knowledge. Many migrant women pay the costs for other family members to migrate and provide them with social ties upon their arrival.

Refugee women and girls or those who are displaced can be forced into situations that lack access to food or other forms of security, and they might be subject to sexual violence or exploitation. The trafficking of women and girls for prostitution and forced labour is a major area of international criminal activity (UN DESA, Division for the Advancement of Women, 2004). Trafficked women frequently originate from regions where there are few employment opportunities for women and they are dependent on others to travel. Many are lured into migrating under the pretence that they will be employed in legitimate occupations and will gradually be able to earn further autonomy and legal status after paying off the debt incurred related to travel and visa fees; however, upon arrival to the destination country, they discover themselves to be trapped into forced prostitution, marriage, domestic work, sweatshops and other forms of exploitation (UN DESA, Division for the Advancement of Women, 2004).

Although international instruments have aimed to establish the human rights of migrants, national laws regulating the admission and stay of international migrants often include provisions that negatively impact migrant women, such as preventing them from being accompanied by husbands or children or limiting their ability to achieve family reunification (UN DESA, Division for the Advancement of Women, 2004).

The World Survey on the Role of Women in Development has made a number of recommendations for improving the situation of women who are migrants or refugees as well as trafficking victims, such as calling on countries to ratify and implement the international legal instruments aimed at protecting their human rights and changing discriminatory national provisions accordingly, as well as developing more policies and means for migrant women to gain better access to education, safe housing, health care, and legitimate employment opportunities (UN DESA, Division for the Advancement of Women, 2004). Possible actions to prevent trafficking include developing better employment opportunities for women in the country of origin, as well as providing them with more information on the methods that traffickers use to attract and entrap women and the legal channels open for migration (UN DESA, Division for the Advancement of Women, 2004).

MAJOR DRIVERS OF MIGRATION

Economic constraints

Voluntary migrations are often driven by economic considerations. Although Africa has made some progress in the promotion of human development in terms of more people rising out of extreme poverty and access to education improving, there are still large groups of people who remain disadvantaged. The rates of migration to richer countries from Africa increase with rising economic opportunity, education, and other factors, and they recede once the wage differential between origin and destination countries narrows sufficiently. Migration has been a source of a sustained supply of labour at reasonably constant wages which has fuelled growth in many advanced countries. Many African countries have lower GDPs, thus magnifying the poverty rates. For example, between 1980 and 2,000, the average per capital growth rate in Africa was zero. Thus, migrants perceive that if they migrate to Europe or the UK and can secure a job, their wages increase and their prospects will improve. One critical factor in the process is obtaining further education in the Western world, which enhances the chances of finding stable employment. For the purposes of study, I will focus on education and employment as significant economic factors that drive African migration.

Unemployment and underemployment

Unemployment is among the major crises facing Africa, for a country is only as healthy as its citizens. Although unemployment across sub-Saharan Africa were relatively low at 6.6% as of the end of 2020 (World Bank, 2021), this figure obscures the dire situation in some countries. Unemployment rates in region's two largest economies, Nigeria and South Africa, are among the world's highest at 34.9% and 33.3%, respectively (Trading Economics, 2021). Similarly, high proportions of the adult population are unemployed in Angola (34.1%), Namibia (33.4%), Mozambique (25.4%), Lesotho (24.7%), Rwanda (23.5%), and Senegal (22.6%; Trading Economics, 2021b). The impact of the COVID-19 pandemic has caused the situation to worsen in some areas; for example, in Nigeria the unemployment rate has increased over 20% from an already alarming 14.2% in the last quarter of 2016 (Kazeem, 2017). The shift has been less extreme in the case of Sudan; however, that country has experienced a 4% rise in unemployment from 13.3% to 17.7% in only two years (Trading Economics, 2018, 2021b).

The labour situation is also disheartening for youth on the continent, which has corresponding effects in slowing economic development. The proportion of unemployed individuals between the ages of 15 and 24 in some African countries is a shocking indicator of how severely the African economy is struggling. Although statistics indicate a slow decline in unemployment rates among youth aged 15–24 from 11.7% in 2012 to 10.6% in 2021 (International Labour Organization, 2021), many work informally and remain underemployed and impoverished due to low, often irregular wages and the lack of a social safety net. Moreover, as in the case of the overall regional unemployment rate, the above figure masks drastic differences across the region. For example, the Kenya National Bureau of Statistics (KNBS, 2021) reported that about 16.3% of Kenyans aged 20–24 were unemployed in the first quarter of 2021. The outlook is even worse in West Africa, where there have been reports in Ghana of 3,000 applicants competing for only five positions at companies ('Where Are the Jobs? - Unemployment Reaches Unacceptable Levels'). In Nigeria, as seen in Figure 8, the National Bureau of Statistics (NBS) reported that a quarter of its youth age 15-24 were unemployed in 2017 (Taiwo, 2017), with the rate for university graduates reaching as high as 47% in January 2016 (Kazeem, 2016). However, by the third quarter of 2020, youth unemployment had increased to 42.5% (National Bureau of Statistics, 2021). As seen in Figure 9, in South Africa, unemployment rates for the same age group are at record levels, with a staggering 67.5% of youth lacking jobs in the third quarter of 2021, and 33.5% were not in employment, education or training (NEET; Statistics South Africa, 2021; Trading Economics, 2021a). In these countries, the situation is attributed to the inability of many of the youths to compete in the job market due to a lack of skills, yet as seen in Figure 10, other reports also note that almost half of the 10 million annual graduates of the over 668 universities in Africa are unable to obtain jobs at home ('Unemployment in Africa: No Jobs for 50% Of Graduates,' 2016).

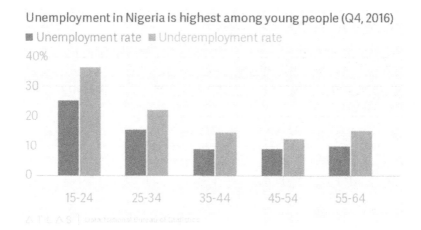

Figure 8. Nigerian unemployment rates, 2016. Reprinted from 'Nigeria's unemployment problem is showing no signs of slowing down,' by Y. Kazeem, 06 June 2017. *Quartz Africa* (https:// qz.com/999641/the-unemployment-rate-in-nigeria-has-climbed-for-nine-consecutive-quarters/). Copyright 2016, Quartz Africa.

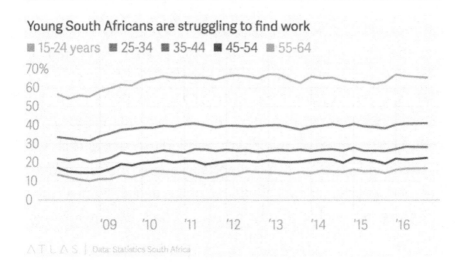

Figure 9. South African unemployment rates, 2016. Reprinted from 'Record unemployment affects these South Africans the most,' by L. Chutel, 2016, 23 November. *Quartz Africa* (https://qz.com/844825/south-africas-unemployment-rate-is-at-a-13-year-high-most-affecting-women-and-the-youth/). Copyright 2016, Quartz.

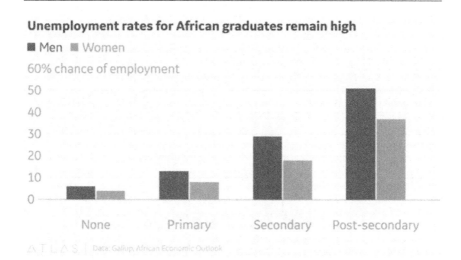

Unemployment rates for African graduates remain high

Figure 10. Unemployment rates among African graduates. Reprinted from 'Technology hubs alone will not create the jobs needed for Africa's youth,' by Quartz marketing team (https://qz.com/476558/technology-hubs-alone-will-not-create-the-jobs-needed-for-africa-youth/). Copyright, n.d., *Quartz*.

EFFECTS OF YOUTH UNEMPLOYMENT

The effects of youth unemployment are manifold. The higher the rate of unemployment, the more difficult it is for youths to partake in economic development. Unemployed youths are unable to use their time adequately and productively, and some turn into either online crime or are integrated into crime by insurgents, such as those youths who are recruited and paid by the Boko Haram insurgents in the Northern part of Nigeria. Others are more prone to rely on their parents, who are themselves often unemployed or underemployed, for sustenance. Parents may pressure unemployed daughters to marry, often resulting in situations of inequality and oppression. If men who marry remain unemployed, parents who can afford to do so are forced to continue to take care of their unemployed child and his wife and children, with the impact producing dependent and irresponsible behaviour in the men.

DOMESTIC VIOLENCE: SPOTLIGHT ON NIGERIA

Domestic violence is a pattern of abusive behaviour in any human relationship that is used by one partner to gain or maintain power and control over another intimate partner. It is not restricted to partners in relationships or in marriage, but can also between a parent and a child, or between siblings. Such experiences are not restricted to any gender but can happen to anyone, and neither is domestic abuse restricted to physical violence, but can rather include emotional, psychological and mental abuse.

The prevalence of intimate-partner violence in sub-Saharan Africa is among the highest in the world, with rates ranging from 30.5% in Nigeria to 43.4% in Zimbabwe; 45.3% in Kenya; 45.5% in Mozambique; 53.9% in Zambia and 57.6% in Cameroun (Bamiwuye & Odimegwu, 2014).

Strong indicators of physical violence include very controlling partners and relationship inequality, such as when the woman is earning more money than her partner. In such cases, high levels of wife beating are attributed to the male partner perceiving himself to lack control within the relationship (Antai, 2011).

Many women feel compelled to tolerate being abused due to social norms that view such behaviour as acceptable; however, the consequences of such violence are extensive— not only does it destroy the morale of the woman and the children who have witnessed it, it also contributes to an ongoing cycle of female inferiority and lack of autonomy. Notably, women who justify wife beating have been found to be more likely to be victims of physical violence (Antai, 2011; Kunnuji, 2014).

Recent studies concluded that two-thirds of Nigerian women have experienced some form of violence during their lifetime, and approximately one-third have experienced domestic violence and intimate partner violence, including battery, torture, acid baths, rape, and death (Eze-Anaba, 2006).

A news article in *The Guardian, Nigeria* reported a recent rise in the prevalence of physical intimate partner violence, whereby a case of a man beating, maiming, or beating his wife occurs at least once a week (Agbedo et al., 2021). In Lagos State alone, the Domestic and Sexual Violence Response Team (DSVRT, 2021d) documents 10,007 cases of domestic and sexual violence involving men, women and children from May 2019 to August 2021. DSVRT (2021a) also notes a rise in cases handled by that agency from 450 in 2016 to 3193 in

2020. For example, whereas 2,584 cases of domestic and sexual violence were reported to that agency (91% of which involved women victims) in 2020 (DSVRT, 2021b), the agency had already taken on 1,617 cases during the first half of 2021 (DSVRT, 2021c).

The high rate of domestic violence against women in Nigeria has become an issue of national concern; however, people in authority have only paid lip service to the issue protecting women and have not enforced existing laws with stiff penalties. Most victims do not report such violations due to general dismissiveness and negative responses from immediate family as well as broader community and society at large (Amnesty Nigeria, 2005). Consequently, a woman who is abused in her family has very little opportunity of obtaining protection from the law. In fact, some victims of domestic violence are mistreated by the courts and many who do pursue their rights are demonised by their husbands and the society.

Acid baths are another form of violence that is increasingly receiving attention in Nigeria. Acid baths are actions of violence where the perpetrator throws acid onto his or her victim's body, resulting in disfigurement, possible loss of eyesight, or death. For example, in 2012, a 25-year-old woman died after being bathed with acid by her former fiancée (Okolie, 2021). More recently, a 40-year-old woman also died after her husband poured acid on her during her sleep (Onuegbu – Uyo, 2020).

Sexual violence is a growing pandemic in Nigeria that has been enormously exacerbated due to the activities of insurgents, bandits, and terrorist groups such as Boko Haram. These groups often use rape and sexual violence against girls and women as a method of ransom negotiation. Boko Haram fighters have committed forms of gender-based violence ranging from rape to sexual slavery, forced marriage, and forced pregnancies (Donald, 2020). Similarly, armed bandits were recently on the rampage in the Shiroro Local Government Area, killing and kidnapping scores of people as well as raping women. The senator for Niger East Senatorial District sent two urgent appeals for intervention to the federal government to halt the carnage (Donald, 2020).

Rape and sexual violence were long perceived as inevitable by-products or spoils of invasion or conquest. However, the international community now recognises that rape and sexual violence is often used as a deliberate criminal strategy to demoralise women and girls. Thus, in 2008, the UN Security Council unanimously passed Resolution 1820 on the use of sexual violence in crisis, indicating that 'rape and other forms of sexual violence can constitute a criminal act, a crime against humanity, or a constitutive act with respect to genocide' (UN Security Council, 2008). This shift in recognition has been significant, as it has allowed for the prosecution of sexual violence against women. Nonetheless, cases of sexual violence remain under-reported due to feelings of shame or stigma among victims. For example, among the 2,279 reported cases of rape and indecent assault in Nigeria in 2017, zero resulted in convictions (Orjinmo, 2020).

Although domestic violence is a violation of fundamental human rights, which the Nigerian constitution claims to uphold, there are nonetheless many provisions that make it legal to engage in domestic violence against women. This stems from the socially accepted idea that men are superior to women and they are therefore allowed to discipline women in any way they deem fit. The subjugation and battering of women in Nigeria is not restricted to the less educated, as statistics report that many educated women who live and work in cities are also regularly assaulted by their husbands. Some Nigerian men may not necessarily hit their wives; rather, they shout, threaten, manipulate, withhold money or sex, and isolate them, among other measures, as a means of punishing them. Some even punish their wives for bearing girls rather than boys, and many will send their sons to school while denying their daughters access to education.

EDUCATION SYSTEMS IN AFRICA

Over the last two decades, education in Nigerian universities have been on a downward spiral due to limited investment by the government, which results in lecturers and other staff being left to work without salaries and under-supported institutional infrastructures. As a consequence, it has become common for the university lecturers to embark on strikes at least once per year in an effort to command the government's attention. Such strikes can last up to or more than four months. Consequently, a four-year course sometimes amounts to a stretch of seven years.

A similar pattern of strikes has permeated other states across Africa. For example, in 2011, the Makerere University in Uganda was closed following strikes by both academic and administrative staff following disputes over pay and pensions, and in 2016, students at South Africa's Durban University of Technology staged country-wide protests over school fees that eventually erupted into violence. Other three South African universities joined in the protests, and the government was forced to shut down four of its universities. The impact of incessant strikes at African universities imposes a financial burden on parents, with students who are mainly from poor backgrounds experiencing the impact, as wealthier parents can opt for other private universities within the country, which are usually very expensive, or they can send their children abroad to Europe, the United States, or other countries in the developed world.

Currently, many African educational institutions at all levels lack the financial resources to deliver a quality learning that is relevant to the 21st century. Some universities do not have up-to-date libraries, and their books are no longer fit for use in developing modern skills. Moreover, states have not always invested in modern technology. For example, some satellite campuses of some Kenyan universities do not have internet access in their libraries. Additionally, the migration of African lecturers to find jobs in countries where they are not overworked for little pay has led to a dearth of top quality academics in many African universities. Besides the added burden of insufficient teachers, some students experience frustration because they are not able to study their preferred courses. Some of the reasons adduced for this in a country like Nigeria is that students from more privileged families are often prioritised to study such courses under a quota system. Moreover, the high level of corruption within the educational system in most schools means that certain students can pay their way into obtaining qualifications thus producing run-of-the-mill graduates, which has led to parents seeking more fail-safe quality education/ certificates for their children abroad (Joseph-Aluko, 2016).

SITUATIONAL AND PROSPECT MIGRATION

As a consequence of these issues, some students have no other choice than to look for other university options elsewhere, which may be within Africa. During the 1980s and 1990s, migration among African students began to intensify, as many universities were still producing graduates, but there were no suitable jobs available for them to apply their skills. Over the past few decades, many migrants have moved out of Africa to different parts of the world in pursuit of further education. Desperate to progress, the migrant may search out opportunities for further education that are not available in his or her country of origin. Unfortunately, many educated migrants may end up settling in developed countries rather than face the dismal prospects of a job search in an underdeveloped economy. This has been the source of the brain drain that has so negatively impacted Africa's development. However, a few migrants in this category fit into the category of what can be called 'prospect migration.' They may travel as 'international students', but are determined to come back to their country of origin, so they can use the skills they have gained in their area of development. Migrants in this category hope to become facilitators of such knowledge and may establish forums or schools, where such training may be further be used for the benefit of their society.

With the UK and US slamming its doors on international migration, African students are diverting their attention to other developed countries in the world. Although the UK has restricted the number of international students who can study in the country, this has not stopped Africans from looking for other options to pursue their education. While the US and UK continue to host around 40,000 English-speaking African students yearly, and France holds the position as the most common destination with over 95,00 students, China has overtaken the former two countries to become the second most popular country for African students studying abroad, with nearly 50,000 students studying there as of 2015 (Breeze & Moore, 2017). The Chinese government has been heavily investing in African education development, and is set to provide about 30,000 scholarships for Africans by 2018

(Breeze & Moore, 2017). It is also important to state that not all students travel out of Africa to study; some travel to other African countries to attend their universities. Ghana had become a university of choice for Nigerians who could not gain admission to their chosen national universities or if the courses they want to study are not available at home. In 2014, for example, it was reported that about 75,000 Nigerians were studying in Ghanaian universities as of 2014 (Fatunde, 2014). As of 2017, about 20,000 South Sudanese university students were studying outside the country, with many are scattered around other universities within Africa, such as in Sudan, Egypt, East Africa and Ethiopia, South Africa, Botswana and Zimbabwe (Kuyok, 2017).

AFRICAN MIGRATION IN THE COVID-19 ERA

The COVID-19 pandemic has had a significant impact on the mobility of migrants, as lockdowns, travel bans, and social distancing brought many societies to a standstill. It is estimated that between March–July 2020, the number of international migrants decreased by 27%, or nearly 2 million, compared with projections based on the numbers between mid-2019 and mid-2020 (UN DESA, 2020). In OECD countries, permanent migration flows are estimated to have fallen by 30% in 2020, labour migration decreased by approximately 24%, temporary labour migration fell by 58%, and the number of new asylum applications dropped by 31% (OECD, 2021). In the context of

Africa, net international migration declined by 2.3 million compared with the five years preceding the pandemic (UN DESA, 2019). The number of migrants from the Horn of Africa traveling to the Gulf countries via Yemen fell by 73% in 2020, from 138,213 to 37,537 (IOM, 2021), and sea departures by sub-Saharan Africans to Europe also sharply decreased (Mixed Migration Centre, 2021). Thousands of sub-Saharan migrants became stranded in transit due to reduced financial resources, the suspension of voluntary return programmes, or border restrictions (Mixed Migration Centre, 2021).

Migrants have also been shown to be more vulnerable to the spread of COVID-19 than the general population. Many migrants experience crowded living and working conditions that expose them to the virus, such as crowded dormitories, refugee camps or factories, and they generally have limited access to healthcare due to poverty and/or undocumented status (Hayward et al., 2020; Wenner et al., 2021). A systematic review found that COVID-19 incidence rates among migrants and refugees were consistently higher than among non-migrant groups (Hintermeier et. al., 2020). Another review similarly indicated that migrants in high-income countries are at increased risk of infection and death due to COVID-19 (Hayward et al., 2020).

Moreover, the pandemic has had a negative impact on economic outcomes for migrants. Migrants have been disproportionately affected by job losses; unemployment rates increased in most OECD countries in 2020, and gaps between foreign- and native-born labour market indicators widened by up to 3 percentage points (OECD, 2021). Job losses have been particularly stark among sub-Saharan African migrants, who have largely been concentrated in service sectors impacted by the lockdowns, such as construction and hospitality, with corresponding impacts in remittances, which saw a reduction of 23% in 2020 and a recovery of only 4% in 2021 (World Bank, 2021a).

CONCLUSIONS

This chapter has examined some basic concepts and theories of migration, as well as the drivers for African migration, with a particular focus on the education situation, which has in turn impacted the numerous economic constraints faced by African societies and the individuals who live in them. While stories of political and conflict refugees abound in Western news reports, in fact, the majority of Africans who migrate to developed countries, including the UK, are related to the search for viable jobs and education options. Although many African universities continue to churn out graduates, there is the challenge that many of the students are unable to use the skills they have gained in the real world. Many African universities are still using older models of teaching to communicate with students, so that much of the knowledge that students gain during their undergraduate coursework cannot be used outside the classroom. The overall educational system in many African institutions is not fit for purpose. Many prospective recruiters have complained that many graduates are unable to produce curriculum vitae, exercise emotional intelligence and demonstrate archaic practices that do not fit into the standard behaviour of the new technologies operating in today's markets. Entrepreneur Fred Swaniker (2017), who heads the African Leadership Academy and the African Leadership University, has argued that in order to truly flourish, Africa needs educational systems that produce graduates who can immediately transfer academic knowledge to the real world and create jobs, rather than useless 'trophy certificate holders,' who lack the skills to help the continent compete in the world economy.

State governments need to create an enabling environment that facilitates the ability of youths to access jobs, such as establishing more vocational schools and colleges. Yet, the process must start with harnessing the potentials of the youths from the time that they are in secondary school. It is unfortunate that even today, many African children do not have access to free primary or secondary school education, resulting in a situation whereby in 2008, nearly 29 million children of primary-school age —54% of them girls —were not in school in sub-Saharan Africa in 2008 (United Nations Educational, Scientific and Cultural Organization (UNESCO), 2017). Ten million African children drop out of primary school every year, so that about 38% of the region's adults—167 million people—still lack basic literacy skills. More than six out of ten of these individuals are women. It is important to point out that universities have often been seen as a male prerogative in many African countries, especially in the 1960s and 1970s, when men were much more likely than women to be encouraged and given opportunities to attend universities, although in a few cases, women could attend teacher training colleges or other secretarial studies and nursing. This has also contributed to the employment and development crises in many countries, whereby female education levels have often lagged behind those of men, and this has been reflected in their employment, income-generating capacity, and overall status in society.

Lack of educational opportunities is at the very root of many of the social, economic and political problems plaguing a number of African countries today. Many of the violent and abusive groups that disrupt civil society are comprised largely of young men and boys who lack access to education or jobs, and those who do receive an education are either ill-equipped to work in the 21st century marketplace, or are forced to sit idly and take on more menial work due to the lack of economic development, which limits the number of skilled jobs available. It is no wonder that so many of Africa's youth and educated adults feel forced to migrate to the developed world to seek their fortunes, yet while those countries benefit from the addition of some the continent's brightest minds, Africa itself continues to lag behind, unable to compete in an increasingly globalised economy.

REFERENCES

Adepoju, A. (1979). Migration and socio-economic change in Africa. International Social Science Journal, 31(2), 207-225.

Agbedo, O., Anazia, D., Awodipe, T., Thomas-Odia, I. & Diamond, M. (2021, 27 February). Domestic violence: Why Nigeria is experiencing an upsurge. Retrieved from https://guardian.ng/saturday-magazine/domestic-violence-why-nigeria-is-experiencing-an-upsurge/

Amin, S. (1995). Migrations in contemporary Africa: A retrospective view. In J. Baker & T.A. Aina. The Migrant Experience in Africa (pp. 29-41). Uppsala: Nordiska Afhkainstitutet

Amnesty International, Nigeria (2005, 31 May). *Unheard voices: Violence Against women in the family*. AFR 44/004/2005, Retrieved from https://www.refworld.org/docid/439463b24.html

Antai, D. (2011). Controlling behaviour, power relations within intimate relationships and intimate partner physical and sexual violence against women in Nigeria. *BMC Public Health*, 11, 511. https://doi.org/10.1186/1471-2458-11-511

Bamiwuye, S.O. & Odimegwu, C. (2014). Spousal violence in sub-Saharan Africa: does household poverty-wealth matter? Reproductive Health, 11: 45, https://doi.org/10.1186/1742-4755-11-45

Breeze, V., & Moore, N. (2017, 30 June). China has overtaken the US and UK as the top destination for Anglophone African students.

Quartz Africa. Retrieved from https://qz.com/1017926/china-has-overtaken-the-us-and-uk-as-the-top-destination-for-anglophone-african-students

Cameron, J., & Dodd, W.A. (1970). *Society, Schools and Progress in Tanzania*. Oxford, UK: Pergamon Press.

Cox D.R. (1972). Regression models and life tables. *Journal of the Royal Statistical Society*, B34 (2), 187–220.

Diop, C.A. (1987). *Pre-colonial Black Africa: A Comparative Study of the Political and Social Systems of Europe and Black Africa, from Antiquity to the Formation of Modern States*. Westport, CT: Lawrence Hill & Co.

Donald, I. (2020, 22 April). Boko Haram, bandits and kidnappers: Rape and sexual violence as tool for negotiation for ransom in Nigeria. *Nigerian Observer*. Retrieved from https://nigerianobservernews.com/2020/04/boko-haram-bandits-and-kidnappers-rape-and-sexual-violence-as-tool-for-negotiation-for-ransom-in-nigeria/

Donnelly, G. (2017, 29 November). What you don't know, but should, about the slave trade happening in Libya right now. *Fortune*. Retrieved from http://fortune.com/2017/11/29/libya-slave-trade/

Ghana Unemployment Rate 1991-2018. (2018). Trading in Economics. Retrieved from https://tradingeconomics.com/ghana/unemployment-rate

Ehrhart, H., Le Goff, M., Rocher, E., & Singh, R. (2014). Does Migration Foster Exports? Evidence from Africa. Policy Research Working Paper 6739. Washington, DC: The World Bank. Retrieved from https://openknowledge.worldbank.org/bitstream/handle/10986/16810/WPS6739.pdf;sequence=1

Elbagir, N., Razek, R., Platt, A., & Jones, B. (2017, 14 November). People for sale: Where lives are auctioned for $400. *CNN World*. Retrieved from https://www.cnn.com/2017/11/14/africa/libya-migrant-auctions/index.html

Eze-Anaba, I. (2006, 07 August). *Domestic violence and legal reforms in Nigeria: Prospects and challenges*. bepress Legal Series. Working Paper 1507. Retrieved from https://law.bepress.com/expresso/eps/1507

Fatunde, T. (2014, 30 May). Focus on Ghana shows 75,000 Nigerians studying there. *University World News*. Retrieved from http://www.universityworldnews.com/article.php?story=20140529173131311

Ferrant, G. & Tuccio, M. (2015). How do female migration and gender discrimination in social institutions mutually influence each other? Working Paper No. 326, OECD Development Centre. Retrieved from https://www.oecd-ilibrary.org/docserver/5js3926d54d7-en.pdf?expires=1554770446&id=id&accname=guest&checksum=53F1213A70284F2C4757184529AEA6B8

Flahaux, M.-L. & De Haas, H. (2016). African migration: trends, patterns, drivers. Comparative Migration Studies, 4, 1. https://doi.org/10.1186/s40878-015-0015-6

Grieco, E. M. and M. Boyd (1998). Women and migration: incorporating gender into international migration theory. Working Paper 98-139, Center for the Study of Population, Florida State University

Hagen-Zanker,J.S. (2008). Why do people migrate? A review of the theoretical literature. MPRA Paper No. 28197. Maastricht Graduate School of Governance, Maastricht University Retrieved from https://mpra.ub.uni-muenchen.de/28197/1/2008WP002

Hagen-Zanker, J.S. (2010). *Modest expectations: Causes and effects of migration on migrant households in source countries* (Doctoral dissertation). Maastricht University. MGSoG Dissertation Series 5. Maastricht, NL: Boekenplan.

Hayward, S. E., Deal, A., Cheng, C., Crawshaw, A., Orcutt, M., Vandrevala, T. F., Norredam, M., Carballo, M., Ciftci, Y., Requena-Méndez, A., Greenaway, C., Carter, J., Knights, F., Mehrotra, A., Seedat, F., Bozorgmehr, K., Veizis, A., Campos-Matos, I., Wurie, F., McKee, M., ... ESCMID Study Group for Infections in Travellers and Migrants (ESGITM) (2021). Clinical outcomes and risk factors for COVID-19 among migrant populations in high-income countries: A systematic review. *Journal of Migration and Health*, 3, 100041. https://doi.org/10.1016/j.jmh.2021.100041

Hintermeier, M., Gencer, H., Kajikhina, K., Rohleder, S., Hövener, C., Tallarek, M., Spallek, J., & Bozorgmehr, K. (2021). SARS-CoV-2 among migrants and forcibly displaced populations: A rapid systematic review. *Journal of Migration and Health*, 4, 100056. https://doi.org/10.1016/j.jmh.2021.100056

Hunwick, J.O. (2003). *Timbuktu and the Songhay Empire: Al-Sadi's Tarikh al-Sudan down to 1613 and other Contemporary Documents*. Leiden, UK: Brill

Hunwick, J.O. & Boye, A.J. (2008). *The Hidden Treasures of Timbuktu: Rediscovering Africa's Literary Culture*. New York, NY: Thames & Hudson

Joseph-Aluko, O. (2016). Africans in the UK, Migration, Integration and Significance. London, UK: Author.

International Labour Organization (2021). Global employment trends for youth 2020: Africa. Retrieved from https://www.ilo.org/wcmsp5/groups/public/---dgreports/---dcomm/documents/briefing note/wcms_737670.pdf

International Organization for Migration (2021, 23 February). IOM: COVID-19 leads to 73% drop in migration from Horn of Africa to Gulf Countries. Retrieved from https://www.iom.int/news/iom-covid-19-leads-73-drop-migration-horn-africa-gulf-countries

Kazeem, Y. (2016, 27 January). About half of the university graduates in Nigeria cannot find jobs. *Quartz Africa*. Retrieved from https://qz.com/603967/about-half-of-the-university-graduates-in-nigeria-cannot-find-jobs/

Kazeem, Y. (2017, 06 June). Nigeria's unemployment problem is showing no signs of slowing down. *Quartz Africa* (https://qz.com/999641/the-unemployment-rate-in-nigeria-has-climbed-for-nine-consecutive-quarters/).

Kenya National Bureau of Statistics (2021). Quarterly labour force report 2021_Quarter_1. Retrieved from https://www.knbs.or.ke/?wpdmpro=quarterly-labour-force-report-2021_quarter_1

Kunnuji, M.O.N. (2014). Experience of domestic violence and acceptance of intimate partner violence among out-of-school adolescent girls in Iwaya community, Lagos state. *Journal of Interpersonal Violence*, 30(4), 543–564.

Kuyok, K.A. (2017, 23 April). South Sudan's overseas students caught between a rock and a hard place. Times Higher Education. Retrieved from https://www.timeshighereducation.com/blog/south-sudans-overseas-students-caught-between-rock-and-hard-place

Lagos State Domestic and Sexual Violence Response Team (2021a). DSVRT annual report comparison of 2016–2020. Retrieved from https://dsvrtlagos.org/infographics/

Lagos State Domestic and Sexual Violence Response Team (2021b). DSVRT reported cases for adults by gender. Retrieved from https://dsvrtlagos.org/infographics/

Lagos State Domestic and Sexual Violence Response Team (2021c, 24 August). Lagos records 1,617 cases of sexual assaults in six months. Retrieved from https://dsvrtlagos.org/2021/08/24/lagos-records-1617-cases-of-sexual-assaults-in-six-months/

Lagos State Domestic and Sexual Violence Response Team (2021d, 02 September). Lagos records over 10,000 cases of domestic, sexual violence in 3 years. Retrieved from https://dsvrtlagos.org/2021/09/02/lagos-records-over-10000-cases-of-domestic-sexual-violence-in-3-years/

Lee, E.S. (1966). A theory of migration. *Demography*, 3(1), 47-57.

Massey, D. S., Arango, J., Hugo, G., Kouaouci, A., Pellegrino, A., & Taylor, J.E. (1998). Worlds in Motion. Oxford, Clarendon Press

McKinney, C.J. (2017, 6 March). Refugees in the UK. Retrieved from https://fullfact.org/immigration/uk-refugees/

Medina of Fez. (1992-2018). *UNESCO World Heritage Centre*. UNESCO. Retrieved from http://whc.unesco.org/en/list/170

Mixed Migration Centre (2021, February). The impact of COVID-19 on refugees and migrants on the move in North and West Africa. Retrieved from https://www.iom.int/sites/g/files/tmzbdl486/files/covid-19_impact_briefing_paper_en.pdf

Momodu, S. (December 2016-March 2017). Africa most affected by the refugee crisis. *Africa Renewal Online*. Retrieved from http://www.un.org/africarenewal/magazine/december-2016-march-2017/africa-most-affected-refugee-crisis

Mora, J., & Taylor, J.E. (2005). Determinants of migration, destination, and sector choice: Disentangling individual, household and community effects. In Ç. Özden & M. Schiff (Eds.), *International Migration, Remittances and Brain Drain* (pp. 21-51). New York: Palgrave Macmillan.

Mosha, R.S. (2000). *The Heartbeat of Indigenous Africa: A Study of the Chagga Educational System*. New York: Garland Publishing, Inc.

Muñiz, O., Li, W., & Schleicher, Y. (2011). Migrant selectivity. Migration conceptual framework: Why do people move to work in another place or country? Retrieved from http://cgge.aag.org/

Migration1e/ConceptualFramework_Jan10/
ConceptualFramework_Jan108.html

Mushi P.A. K. (2009) *History of Education in Tanzania*. Dar-es-Salaam: Dar-es-Salaam University Press.

National Bureau of Statistics (2021). Unemployment Statistics. Retrieved from https://www.nigerianstat.gov.ng/

Nigeria's unemployment rate rises from 14.2% to 18.8%. (2017, 23 December). *Vanguard*. Retrieved from https://www.vanguardngr.com/2017/12/nigerias-unemployment-rate-rises-14-2-18-8/

OECD (2021, 28 October). *International migration outlook 2021*. Retrieved from https://www.oecd.org/migration/international-migration-outlook-1999124x.htm

Okolie, I. (2012, 20 December). Acid bath victim, Chika Egbo dies. *Vanguard*, Retrieved from https://www.vanguardngr.com/2012/12/acid-bath-victim-chika-egbo-dies/

Onuegbu – Uyo, C. (2020, 14 October). Police arrest Akwa Ibom man over death of 40-year-old wife. *Vanguard*. Retrieved from https://www.vanguardngr.com/2020/10/police-arrest-akwa-ibom-man-over-death-of-40-year-old-wife/

Orjinmo, N. (2020, 05 June). #WeAreTired: Nigerian women speak out over wave of violence. *BBC News*. Retrieved from https://www.bbc.com/news/world-africa-52889965

Shimeles, A. (2018). Understanding the patterns and causes of African migration: Some facts,' by A. Shimeles. In B.S. Coulibaly

(Ed.), Foresight Africa: Top priorities for the Continent in 2018 (pp. 54-57). Washington, D.C.: The Brookings Institution. Retrieved from https://www.brookings.edu/wp-content/uploads/2018/01/ foresight-2018_full_web_final1.pdf

Shimeles, A. and T. Nabasaga. (2018). Why is inequality high in Africa. *Journal of African Economies*, forthcoming.

Smith, D.D. (1992). APA: *The Ruin of a Nation Begins in The Homes of Its People*. Washington, DC: American Red Cross. Retrieved from https://resource.nlm.nih.gov/luna/servlet/detail/ NLMNLM~1~1~101455760~159739

Statistics South Africa (2021). Quarterly labour force survey, Quarter 3: 2021. Retrieved from http://www.statssa.gov.za/ publications/P0211/P02113rdQuarter2021.pdf

Swaniker, F. (2017, 21 September). African universities: education with a purpose. *New African*. Retrieved from http:// newafricanmagazine.com/african-universities-education-purpose/

Taiwo, S. (2017, 6 June). More Nigerian graduates become jobless, unemployment rate hits 21%. *The Pulse*. Retrieved from http:// www.pulse.ng/bi/politics/unemployed-nigerians-more-nigerian- graduates-become-jobless-unemployment-rate-hits-21- id6790778.html

Tharoor, I. (2017, 29 November). A 'slave auction' puts the global spotlight back on Libya. *Washington Post*. Retrieved from https:// www.washingtonpost.com/news/worldviews/wp/2017/11/29/a- slave-auction-puts-the-global-spotlight-back-on-libya/

Trading Economics (2018). Sudan - Economic Indicators. Retrieved from https://tradingeconomics.com/sudan/indicators

Trading Economics (2021a). South Africa unemployment rate. Retrieved from https://tradingeconomics.com/south-africa/unemployment-rate

Trading Economics (2021b). Unemployment rate: Africa. Retrieved from https://tradingeconomics.com/country-list/unemployment-rate?continent=africa

UN DESA (2020). *World population prospects 2019*. Retrieved from https://population.un.org/wpp/Download/Standard/Migration/

UN DESA (2020). *International migration 2020*. Retrieved from https://www.un.org/development/desa/pd/news/international-migration-2020

UN DESA Division for the Advancement of Women (2004). 2004 *World survey on the role of women in development: Women and international migration*. Retrieved from https://www.un.org/womenwatch/daw/public/WorldSurvey2004-Women&Migration.pdf

UN DESA Population Division (2013). International migration report 2013. Retrieved from https://www.un.org/en/development/desa/population/publications/pdf/migration/migrationreport2013/Full_Document_final.pdf

UN DESA Population Division (2015, December). *Trends in international migration*, 2015. Retrieved from https://www.un.org/en/development/desa/population/migration/publications/

populationfacts/docs/MigrationPopFacts20154.pdf

UN Security Council. (2008). UN Security Council resolution 1820 on women, peace and security. Retrieved from https://www.unwomen.org/en/docs/2008/6/un-security-council-resolution-1820

Wenner, J., Biddle, L., Gottlieb, N., & Bozorgmehr, K. (2021). Inequalities in access to healthcare by local policy model among newly arrived refugees: evidence from population-based studies in two German states. MedRxiv. doi: https://doi.org/10.1101/2021.07.13.2126024m

World Bank (2021a). *COVID-19 crisis through a migration lens.* Migration and Development Brief 32. Retrieved from https://openknowledge.worldbank.org/bitstream/handle/10986/33634/COVID-19-Crisis-Through-a-Migration-Lens.pdf?sequence=5&isAllowed=y

World Bank (2021b). Unemployment, total (% of total labour force) (modeled ILO estimate) - Sub-Saharan Africa. Retrieved from Unemployment, total (% of total labour force) (modeled ILO estimate) - Sub-Saharan Africa

7

AFRICAN MIGRATION AND SIGNIFICANCE: PERSPECTIVE OF KENYA HEALTH SECTOR

Martha Nyawira Chege

Kenya is increasingly experiencing a double burden of disease whereby non-communicable diseases (NCDs) are being reported at nearly the same level as communicable diseases. Common NCDs reported in private hospitals include hypertension and hypertensive crises and diabetes with kidney complications. Cancer is increasingly being reported in both private and public facilities. The most reported communicable conditions are community acquired pneumonia with complications, HIV/AIDS, malaria, and diarrhoea in children under 5 years. Service provision in both private and public hospitals is affected when health workers depart for 'greener pastures', as the resulting strain on remaining personnel leaves them demotivated. Some personnel have chosen to pursue further training such that they qualify for lecturing jobs which offer more flexible work schedules, thereby resulting in an even leaner workforce available to directly attend to patients.

The true test of Kenya's health sector capacity came with the coronavirus disease (COVID-19). When the first case was announced in Kenya on March 13, 2020, the Ministry of Health rolled out various measures in an attempt to control its spread and avoid overwhelming the health system. Health workers from various sections, including those on leave, were recalled for training and redeployment to various response points. All cadres of health service providers from community health volunteers to section directors were redistributed to attend to the preventive, control and curative aspects of COVID-19 management. As has occurred worldwide, inadequate personal protective equipment (PPE) was a serious challenge in those cities located at pandemic epicentres during the early days of the disease response. A few health workers and other support staff working within the health facilities were exposed, and some were confirmed as positive cases. This threat to the workers sent healthcare managers back to the drawing board to upgrade the preparedness and response protocols. Some county governments went further in their consideration for additional risk allowance to the frontline health workers. Amid concerns about a large-scale outbreak in the country, the government also invited applications for additional health workers to be absorbed into the public health system. Thankfully, the disease appears to have been controlled.

Kenya's ability to contain the COVID-19 pandemic is largely attributable to the dynamic disease surveillance and contact tracing systems that were put in place even before outbreak.

The existing community health strategy that forms the first level (Level 1) of the health care system in Kenya has played a vital role in contact tracing and disseminating preventive health messages at the household level. The health sector has worked closely with the interior security and coordination structures to enhance contact tracing and surveillance of those on quarantine as well as to ensure the enforcement of other control measures such as the dusk-to-dawn curfew. Reports showing up to 67% asymptomatic cases reinforce the critical importance of preventive measures such as effective contact tracing, proper hygiene—including mass usage of masks, physical distancing and mass testing to determine the actual level of the population exposed to the disease. Over time, we have seen local industries and institutions adapt their production lines to provide additional PPEs and ventilators to ameliorate shortages.

The 2015 Kenya Health Workforce Report indicated that the country has only a total of 5,660 medical doctors to serve the entire population of about 46 million. This is by far lower than the recommended physician-to-population ratio of 1:1000. Kenya's population grows by more than 3,200 daily, which far exceeds the rate at which new doctors are added to the market annually. However, Kenya is currently experiencing greater growth in the number of healthcare workers due to an increase in training institutions. Medical schools have increased from two in 2006 to 10 today, and nursing schools increased from 77 to 102 during the same period.

The Kenyan government is no longer directly absorbing health workers who have recently completed their internships into the system. The national referral hospitals still have the highest number of specialized health workers among public health facilities; however, with the devolution of health services from the national to the county level, the public health sector has experienced a shift in the process of recruiting, training and general management of its health workers. The change is becoming more apparent as existing facilities are upgraded or new ones constructed to meet unique county-level needs. Unwilling to work at county facilities, many young people are seeking jobs in local private hospitals or pursuing work outside the country. Those with special care training (critical care, paediatric/neonatal, peri-operative, anaesthetist, accident & emergency, cardiology, orthopaedic, nephrology, ophthalmic, radiology, and psychiatry) may choose to remain in the facilities where they trained—which may be abroad, as some local private hospitals train their health workers in India or Pakistan—or work in private hospitals, even on locum basis. All in all, there needs to be a re-alignment of the entire health system so that those who are trained are retained within the counties for the benefit of the country at large.

WHY THE MIGRATION?

Beginning in the late 1990s–mid-2000s, Kenya experienced a huge exodus of health workers, especially to the United States,

Australia, and the United Kingdom. Some African countries also received health workers, albeit at a smaller scale, including South Africa, Botswana and Rwanda. The movement has led to a massive loss of trained, highly skilled and experienced personnel from both private and public health facilities, and the main affected cadres have been nurses, doctors and nutritionists. Human psychology may be a factor in the shift, as those who have moved perceive those other countries offer better working conditions and pay, with consequently improved livelihoods for themselves and their extended families who receive remittances. Those who have gone ahead and settled abroad also serve as channels for their friends and families to obtain job opportunities and/or citizenship in those countries. Although the outflow began to slow in 2008 due to the global financial crisis, the gaps created in health facilities across the country have never really been filled.

Some of the main causes for the migrations were unfavourable working terms and conditions in both private and public hospitals. Individual concerns raised to management generally went unanswered due to the lack of labour unions to represent health workers. Long working hours, poorly equipped public facilities and low pay put a strain on individuals, and some took advantage of offers by various recruiting agencies to sign up for work abroad. Later, unions were formed for the main cadres (nurses and doctors) to lobby for better working conditions; however, many of their demands have yet to be met.

As the country has grappled with increasing incidences of NCDs, some hospitals, especially from India, have partnered with local hospitals or set up shop in Kenya while referring complicated cases to the parent hospital for further management. One side effect of these new developments is that the lack of operational capacity for procedures such as liver and bone marrow transplants may lead some health workers in Kenya to train outside the country, where they are likely to remain in order to be able to practice in their specialised areas.

SIGNIFICANCE OF HEALTH WORKER MIGRATION

A positive effect of the mass exodus a decade ago is the opportunities created for fresh graduates to obtain jobs, for those in service to earn promotions, and for others to enter into medical training. Amidst severe shortages in the health sector, an increasing number of young people in are being trained in Kenyan medical colleges and universities. While this in itself is good, some may not be joining the profession due to a vocational calling, but rather because it appears to be more lucrative career.

Women have equal opportunities for training and career advancement. The only challenge that may affect women more than men is if they need to train away from home for extended periods of time, which may be hindered by family interests. Working professionals with families have to manage their marriages and children along with their jobs. While some may initially have to leave their spouses and children behind, others may end up separating for a long time, causing relational strains with both their immediate and extended families.

Domestic violence affecting the general society has not spared the health care providers. The fact that many households in Kenya are headed by women is partly due to separations to escape domestic violence. Some individuals might end up seeking for opportunities abroad to escape family issues, although many may not openly admit this.

Contributions: [1]Joyce Wangari Mukui, Kenya Registered Critical Care Nurse (Higher Diploma), joyce_mukui@yahoo.com

[2]Franklin Gachemi Ndirangu, Medical Officer (MBchB [Moi], MBA [Edinburgh]), frankndirangu@gmail.com

BIOGRAPHY

Martha Nyawira Chege

Martha Nyawira Chege is a public health specialist with a bias towards public health nutrition. She is passionate about contributing to the prevention and/ or management of both communicable and non-communicable diseases. Martha's experience is in managing diverse health programmes with skills in training, administration, planning and coordination of programmes. She is exceptional at capacity building of health workers, health education to communities, implementation of health campaigns, coordination of stakeholders and technical working groups, and development of content for strategic frameworks and policy briefs. She enjoys working in teams, and is keen to learn from others and volunteer her time and energy towards the corporate good.

Connect with Martha: Email: chegeress@gmail.com LinkedIn: https://www.linkedin.com/in/martha-chege-3379b83b/

8

AN OVERVIEW OF

RETURN MIGRATION TO GHANA

Olivia Bola J-Olajide Aluko

ABSTRACT

Purpose:

This paper examines the phenomenon of migration and returns in Ghana.

Design/Methodology approach

Following a review of historical migration trends in Ghana, the paper discusses return migration, distinguishing between the experiences of voluntary and forced returnees.

Results

Ghana has historically experienced population in- and outflows; however, the latter have intensified over the past 60 years. Ghana has West Africa's highest emigration rate for highly skilled workers, and the country has repeatedly introduced initiatives aimed at attracting returnees to contribute to economic development. However, many unskilled workers have been subject to forced return due to deportation, and they face significant challenges reintegrating into Ghanaian social and economic life.

Originality/Value

Return migration is increasingly a focus of study; however, limited research has examined the challenges faced by forced returnees.

Keywords

Migration, return migration, Ghana, brain drain

BACKGROUND

People migrate in search of better lives, new jobs, or education opportunities and/or as a result of political and economic changes and crises. Some migrants ultimately return to their country of origin, where those who are highly skilled can stimulate or support knowledge-based economic development. Such return migrations can contribute to reverse the adverse effects of brain drain in developing and newly industrialising countries (Iredale and Guo, 2001; Hunger, 2004).

From 1980 to 2010, the number of African migrants doubled

to reach 30.6 million, and while approximately half remained on the continent, the proportion of extra-regional movements have steadily increased over time (World Bank, 2014). Over the past four decades, a growing number of African professionals have migrated to more developed regions such as Europe, North America, and Canada. Among the countries affected by this brain drain, Ghana had the highest emigration rates for highly skilled workers in West Africa in 2009 at 46%, including more than 56% of doctors and 24% of nurses (International Organisation for Migration [IOM], 2009).

This paper focuses on the migration phenomenon in Ghana with a particular focus on return migration. Following a general discussion of migration trends, I discuss issues related to both voluntary and forced return migration in the country.

MIGRATION TRENDS

Population movements are not a strange phenomenon in Ghana. Most ethnic groups in Ghana have oral traditions that ascribe their origins to other African regions, and people have historically moved from Ghana to other African regions for trading purposes (Amenumey, 1986; Drucker-Brown, 1986; Meyerowitz, 1958; Wilks, 1981). Prior to the trans-Atlantic slave trade, the trans-Saharan caravan routes are among the earliest evidence of significant interaction between West and North Africa for trading and scholarly exchange (Boahen, 1966). From the 1400s onwards, north-south movements of people and goods were interrupted following the arrival of the Europeans on the West African coast. New patterns of movement within the sub-region and the rest of the world began to emerge through the slave trade and colonization (Boahen 1966). This development increased the scale of movements in Ghana, which has remained the case into the present.

Until the late 1960s, Ghana was a net immigration destination for individuals from other African countries (TwumBaah et al. 1995). However, political instability and economic downturns in the late 1960s and early 1970s led to the expulsion of 250,000 migrants, most of whom were of West African origin, and the proportion of foreigners in Ghana decreased from 12.3 % in 1960 to 6.6 % in 1970 (Anarfi et al. 2003). Continued economic decline throughout the 1970s until the mid -1980s sparked waves of emigration that created a diaspora spanning Europe, North America, the Middle East, and Asia as well as intensified regional migration, particularly to Nigeria and Ivory Coast. A broader category of labour emigration began with skilled workers and professionals; however, by the early 1980s, many unskilled and semi-skilled workers had also begun to leave (Anarfi et al. 2003; Schaans et al., 2013). This emigration had a negative effect on the country's development, as the migrants' absence resulted in a loss of capital and the destruction of the regional trading nexus as well as the disruption of the social fabric of communities (Amponsah, 2016; Brydon, 1985).

During the first half of the 1980s, there was a mass expulsion of Ghanaian migrants from Nigeria, which significantly altered the West African migration order, as many chose to migrate to other regions of Africa as well as Europe and North America rather than return home. By the mid-1990s, an estimated 2-4 million Ghanaians, or 10-20% of the population, lived abroad (Akyeampong 2000; Anarfi et al. 2003).

RETURN MIGRATION

Return migration is defined by the **International Organisation for Migration (IOM 2019) as the act or process of returning to the point of departure. It** ranges from spontaneous voluntary to voluntary assisted, and deportation/forced return. Types of return migration also include cyclical/ seasonal return, return from short- or long-term migration, and repatriation.

In some cases, **migrants or their descendants have return**ed to Ghana by their own choice, often after a significant period abroad (e.g., IOM, 2020). Return migration has been factored into the Ghanaian development discourse and planning, especially since the 1990s. To advance development, Ghana has initiated programmes to encourage the return of both Ghanaians abroad and 'friends of Ghana'. For example, the Emancipation Day celebrations in the 1990s were aimed at helping African Americans and people of African descent to return to Africa and Ghana, and the Homecoming Summit in

2001 was implemented to harness the skills and resources of Ghanaians in the diaspora to help with national development (Ankomah et al. 2012; Hasty, 2019). More recently, Ghanaian president Nana Akufo-Addo announced 2019 as the 'Year of Return' in an initiative intended to encourage Africans in the Diaspora to settle and invest in Ghana (King, 2020; Larnaud, 2020). However, diaspora returnees often underestimate the level of self-determination needed to transplant oneself to a country to which they are rooted but have been disconnected by the enslavement process. Similarly, more recent returnees often encounter difficulties re-integrating into their communities. Many have been unprepared for the challenges this kind of move can bring, and some have ended up moving back to North America or Europe (Arhin-Sam, 2019; Kleist, 2017, 2018). Returnee labour migrants often experience difficulties due to family demand and unemployment, and many have not accumulated sufficient savings to build prosperous lives (Issifu, 2018). However, returnees who have accumulated savings and acquired western values, attitudes and ideas often experience improved social networks and become highly influential in local decision-making in their localities (Yendaw, 2013).

Forced return migration occurs when people are returned to their place of departure, often due to breaches such as failure to provide the necessary immigration credentials at the point of arrival or violating immigration rules in the country of destination. Many Ghanaians have been expelled from Europe and North America due to the tightening of immigration laws and restrictions on traveling abroad, particularly in European countries that require the possession of valid travel and employment documents (Anarfi et al. 2003; Kleist 2017, 2018). In the US, deportations have significantly increased since the election of President Donald J. Trump, as regulations have become stricter and fewer entry visas have been granted. For example, the number of Ghanaians deported more than tripled from 94 in 2016 to 305 in 2017, and 751 Ghanaians were removed from 2017-2019 after being convicted of various offences, including acts that undermined border control and the integrity of the US immigration system (U.S. Immigration and Customs Enforcement 2017, 2019). Similarly, in the last three years, more charter flights have been carrying Ghanaians from the U.K. to their country of origin. Moreover, in the wake of the Covid-19 pandemic, the rates of Ghanaians deported or 'repatriated' to Ghana have increased as countries close their borders ('224 Ghanaians repatriated from the UK, decry conditions', 2020).

Before a person is deported, he/she is generally cut off from the outside world and detained in a detention centre. Thus, it is difficult for them to make arrangements to pick up any property or monies before they are deported, and by the time of their arrival in Ghana, they may have little or no money with them. Little done by the government to help returnees reintegrate into Ghanaian society; however, the IOM is vested with the responsibility of providing assistance to Ghanaians and others who are returning to their homelands. The organization supports recent arrivals to Ghana who are voluntary returnees and those who have been deported with a sum of 440 Ghana cedis to meet their immediate needs. Overall, depending on the support on the ground, it may take from six months to 12 months or more to achieve any economic recovery, particularly if the returnee aims to start a business.

A deportee may be fortunate to have understanding family members who are empathetic to the deportee's psychological trauma and may be able to offer them accommodation or a loan to start a business. However, such support is rare because many deportees have caught ties with their relatives or may not want them to discover that he/she was forcefully returned to their homelands. Similarly, many deportees cannot turn to friends for assistance because they may not necessarily have been in touch before the sudden return; moreover, their friends may not be in a position to provide support. In Ghana, it is considered shameful to return home with empty hands, as migrants are expected to return as wealthy benefactors rather than need the help of those family and friends who have been expecting their support.

CONCLUSION

Population movements have existed in Ghana from the beginning of its history; however, the country has experienced an intensification outflows during the past sixty years. In recent decades, some migrants have returned to Ghana for various reasons. On the one hand, the country has sought to attract its educated and skilled workers who have departed for more developed regions. In addition, the unique phenomenon of the return of diasporic Africans who are descendants of forced emigrants to Ghana, many of whom have been invited to assist with the economic development. On the other hand, other returnees have been deported from their destination countries and are forced to return home with limited resources. Whereas the former two categories often enjoy high levels of prestige and enhanced social networks, the latter face failed expectations and often experience significant challenges reintegrating into their communities. As the Covid-19 pandemic forces more such returns, it is critical that returnees be provided with economic and social assistance to support their reintegration.

REFERENCES

224 Ghanaians repatriated from the UK, decry conditions.2020 19 June. *Africa Briefing*, https://africabriefing.org/2020/06/224-ghanaians-repatriated-from-the-uk-decry-conditions/

Akyeampong, E. 2000. Africans in the Diaspora: the Diaspora and Africa. *African Affairs*, 99(395), 183–215.

Amenumey, D.E.K. 1986. *The Ewe in pre-colonial times: a political history with special emphasis on the Anlo, Ge, and Krepi*. Sedco Pub. Ltd.

Amponsah , Y.A. 2016. *An assessment of initiatives to combat the brain drain in Ghana*. MA thesis, University of the Witwatersrand, Johannesburg.

Anarfi, J., Kwankye, S., Ababio, O. and Tiemoko, R. 2003. *Migration from and to Ghana: A background paper*. Development research centre on Migration, Globalization and Poverty, Working paper C4, University of Sussex.

Ankomah, P., Larson, T., Roberson, V., & Rotich, J. (2012). A creative approach to development: The case for active engagement of African diaspora in Ghana. *Journal of Black Studies* 43(4), 385-404.

Arhin-Sam, K. 2019. *Return migration, reintegration and sense of belonging: the case of skilled Ghanaian returnees*. Nomos Verlag.

Boahen, A.A. 1966. *Topics in West African history*. London: Longman's.

Brydon, L. 1985. Ghanaian responses to the Nigerian expulsions of 1983. *African Affairs*, 84(337), 561-585.

Clemens M. and G. Pettersson. 2007 *New data on African health professionals abroad*. Working Paper No. 95. Washington DC. : Center for Global Development

Docquier, F. and A. Marfouk. 2006. International migration by educational attainment (1990-2000). In C. Ozden and M. Schiff (Eds*), International migration, remittances and development*. New York: Palgrave Macmillan and World Bank.

Drucker-Brown, S. .1986. The story of Magazi Akushi: the origin of the Gambaga, Mamprusi Muslims, Northern Region, Ghana. *Cambridge Anthropology* 11(1): 78-83.

Ehrhart, H., Le Goff, M., Rocher, E. and Singh, R.J. 2014. *Does migration foster exports? Evidence from Africa.* World Bank Policy Research Working Paper 6739. Available from https://openknowledge.worldbank.org/bitstream/handle/10986/16810/WPS6739.pdf?sequence=1

Hasty, J. 2019. Rites of passage, routes of redemption: emancipation tourism and the wealth of culture. *Africa Today* 49 (3),47-76.

Hunger, U. 2004. Brain gain: Theoretical considerations and empirical data on a new research perspective in development and migration theory. *IMIS-Beiträge* 24, 213-221.

International Organization for Migration. 2019. 2019 Return and reintegration: Key highlights. https://publications.iom.int/books/2019-return-and-reintegration-key-highlights

International Organization for Migration. 2020. IOM Assists over 1,400 migrants with voluntary return to Ghana. https://www.iom.int/news/iom-assists-over-1400-migrants-voluntary-return-ghana

Iredale, R.R. and Guo. 2001. *The transforming role of skilled and business returnees: Taiwan, China and Bangladesh*. Wollongong: Centre for Asia Pacific Social Transformation Studies.

Issifu, 2018. Empirical investigation of impediments to returnees' entrepreneurship in Ghana: An application of structural equation modelling. *Mediterranean Journal of Social Sciences* 9(1), 155-170.

King, T. 2020 4 August. Ghana Looks to Long Relationship With African Americans for Investment. Council for Foreign Relations. https://www.cfr.org/blog/ghana-looks-long-relationship-african-americans-investment

Kleist, N. 2017. Disrupted migration projects: the moral economy of involuntary return to Ghana from Libya. *Africa: The Journal of the International African Institute* 87(2), 322-342.

Kleist, N. 2018. Trajectories of involuntary return migration to Ghana: Forced relocation processes and post-return life. *Geoforum*, https://doi.org/10.1016/j.geoforum.2017.12.005

Larnaud, N. 2020. "This is your home — come here and makes it yours": Ghana encourages African Americans to visit as part of the "Year of Return" campaign.*CBS News*, January 27. https://www.cbsnews.com/news/this-is-your-home-come-here-and-make-it-yours-heres-how-ghanas-year-of-return-has-impacted-african-americans/

Meyerowitz, E.L.R., 1958, The Akan of Ghana: Their ancient beliefs, Faber and Faber Ltd., London.

Organization of Economic Cooperation and Development 2004. International mobility of the highly skilled: from statistical analysis to the formulation of policies. Paris: OECD.

Schans, D., Mazzucato, V., Schoumaker , B., Flahaux, M-L. 2013. Changing patterns of Ghanaian Migration. International Migration Institute.

Twum-Baah, K. A., Nabila, J.S. and Aryee, A.F. 1995. *Migration research study in Ghana*. Accra: Ghana Statistical Service.

U.S. Immigration and Customs Enforcement 2017. Fiscal year 2017 ICE enforcement and removal operations report. Available at https://www.ice.gov/sites/default/files/documents/Report/2017/iceEndOfYearFY2017.pdf

U.S. Immigration and Customs Enforcement 2019. Fiscal year 2019 enforcement and removal operations report. Available at https://www.ice.gov/sites/default/files/documents/Document/2019/eroReportFY2019.pdf

Wilks, I. .1981. The Mossi and the Akan states to 1800. In J.F.A. Ajayi and M. Crowder, editors, *History of West Africa*. UK: Longman Group Limited, pp. 413-455.

Yendaw, E. 2013. Does international migration represent a mechanism for status enhancement or status loss? A study of international return migrants to Ghana. American Research Institute for Policy Development.

9

THE CHALLENGES OF
AFRICAN IDENTITY IN THE UK

Joseph Adamson

To this day, the term 'Black' evokes memories for many people of African descent due to the evils of slavery and colonisation coupled with the knowledge that so many of the young men and women who were potential catalysts to African development were uprooted and dispersed to Britain and its colonies in North America and the Caribbean.

Enslaved individuals who were brought to the UK during the Trans-Atlantic trade were forced to adopt new names and acclimate to a culture at variance with their identities. Based on this history, it is unsurprising that the current generation of Black people is growing up without a sense of identity or attachment to their origins. Indeed, many Black Africans today have disassociated themselves from other people of their race; many lack any substantive links to Africa due to ignorance and misconceptions about the continent and confusion regarding their racial identities.

People of African descent also trace their roots to the Caribbean and other parts of the world. Although I am aware of the challenges experienced by these people, this short essay is focused on Africans living in the UK, as my own perspective derives from my own African origin and that of the large population of Africans in the UK.

Africans in the UK are subject to the terminology used to define us. Regardless of origin, Africans are divided into 'Black Minority and Ethnic' (BME) and 'Black Asian and Minority Ethnic' (BAME) groups. Such descriptions are currently used for completing all forms and serve as part of the ethnic monitoring system used by most organisations in the UK.

The problem with this categorisation is that Black Africans are not a homogenous or uniform group, but rather a diverse collection of groups with different customs, cultures and languages. Attempts to encompass us under a uniform category overlook the difficulties of working together for the same cause.

Currently, there are varied groups of Africans residing in the UK. Some have inherited British citizenship, whereas others can be classified into second, third, and fourth-generation residents. Later-generation descendants who were not born in Africa may experience challenges integrating with native Africans while also struggling to be accepted by other British. Although their parents or grandparents are Africans, these individuals identify as British and have no connection with Africa (Collier, 1991). Not all Black people identity as

190

'Africans', and they object to any suggestion that they are 'Africans' by virtue of their roots.

The historical roots of these identity conflicts derive from the colonial era. For over three hundred years, Europeans created a hostile environment that created division and constrained the growth and development of African societies. Before the colonial period, Africans traded among themselves without the hindrance of borders (Lester, 2001). Africa has not recovered since the continent was partitioned during the Berlin conference of 15 November1884, and ethnic conflicts between tribes and states have led to escalating wars.

Currently, people from all of Africa's 54 countries live in the UK, especially in London; however, there is no single identity that unites them as Africans, and there is no central community that showcases Africa and its people in the UK. Rather, what we have are small, diverse community groups centred on nationalities. It can be argued that regardless of any individual successes, efforts toward large-scale progress will compromised in the absence of a strong, unified community.

Africans have qualifications across vital professions; however, we struggle to translate our expertise into economic empowerment for our community. Whereas a growing minority within the African community can claim successes, other Black Africans are mired in low-income jobs and poverty. It appears that many Africans are concerned with gaining individual success and being seen as achievers;

however, they struggle to translate this into community development. There are no community banks within the Black African community in the UK, nor are there schools or colleges other than nursery schools owned by Black Africans.

CONCLUSION

One can conclude that Africans are concerned with diverse priorities. Very few Africans are interested in community development; rather, we devote the bulk of our time and money to religious institutions. Sadly, this is one of the problems affecting the African community. As a result, there are very few community initiatives in place that can absorb youths who experience problems without resorting to government funding. The African community must invest in education designed for people of African origin, particularly youths, who face many challenges in the UK, including poor self-esteem and identity crises. Celebrating Black History Month every October is not sufficient to provide an education for the young people.

Africans living in the UK must come together and form a strong community regardless of their region of origin. We must know and remember that African have been living in the UK for the last 500 years or more, however mainstream media never mentions this fact. Instead the focus is on how African is poor and less educated we are. The African stories are always distorted. Now we are in the 21st century there is no time to wait for anyone to do things for us.

The media is driving rapid changes in the world, and this is another area that currently needs attention. At present, there are two television stations and a handful of Internet radio stations that serve selective audiences. Entrepreneurs must collaborate to form a professional media platform to represent Africans in the UK. The situation will not improve if Africans in the UK fail to unite (Perham, 1951).

BIOGRAPHY

Joseph Adamson

Joseph Adamson Studied at West London University [Thames Valley University] BA [Hons] Audio Technology. Joseph is the CEO and founder of Africans In London TV [AILTV]. Joseph is very passionate about African identity and origin. Joseph created the AILTV to entertain, to inform, to educate but also to explore and document the progress and the challenges of people of African origin. Over the last ten years AILTV has been creating programmes that speaks directly to the people of African origin.

PART 3

Essays on

Realising Africa's Potentials

10

FROM BRAIN DRAIN

TO BRAIN GAIN

Ademola Adeoye

For the last 20 years, I have consistently laboured to struggle against the monster of 'brain drain' that has been bedevilling Africa for decades and holding us back from taking our rightful place on the world stage.

Africa exports its best brains to the Western world while its own house is left in ruins. Zambia once had approximately 2000 medical doctors; however, I do not think that more than 800 currently remain. Similarly, Kenya retains only 10% of the nurses and doctors trained there. Why is this happening? The reality is that medical practitioners are more valued beyond the continent, and Western countries provide many basic amenities that are lacking in Africa. In order to retain our best medical practitioners, we need to place a higher value on them that they are currently accorded in the Western world. We need to make this continent a place where they can thrive rather than merely survive.

In Nigeria, the petroleum industry hires thousands of skilled expatriates despite the fact that we can find people with similar skills within Nigeria and elsewhere on this continent. Rather than developing our own manpower, we allow talented individuals to grow wings and fly to the Western world, where they are further trained, valued and profitably deployed.

During the Agricultural Age, the young and strong were forced into slavery because the US economy needed strong hands to pick cotton. However, the current Information Age requires the best and brightest rather than the young and strong, and our most talented people are being lured away with visas and green cards. How do we retain our best in Nigeria during this Information Age?

On the 30th of August, 2016, Mark Zuckerberg made his first trip to Nigeria. During his visit, he did not travel to the seats of power in Lagos or Abuja, but rather made his way to the 'CcHUB' at Yaba, our own budding Silicon Valley. Before he departed Nigeria for Kenya, Zuckerberg made a profound statement: 'Nigeria will shape the world'. What did Zuckerberg envision as the basis for our future growth? He saw technological knowledge!

If we can build on the solid foundation that the emerging 'tech-savvy' generation has laid and make Nigeria and Africa as a whole more habitable, then the best and brightest of our people shall be retained and those in the diaspora shall be attracted back home.

African leaders need to understand that knowledge is the engine that drives economic growth and we cannot eliminate poverty without first nurturing and growing our intellectual capital. Without technological knowledge, Africans shall continue to suffer economically.

In summary, as a people, we can move from 'brain drain' to 'brain gain' if we increase and nurture our intellectual capital, make Africa habitable for our best brains, value them more than they are valued in the Western world, and productively and maximally deploy them.

BIOGRAPHY

Ademola Adeoye

Ademola Adeoye is the lead pastor, Faith For The Nations Christian Centre, Ikeja, Lagos, Nigeria, West Africa and he is the CEO of the World-Class Impact Network Limited, a well-structured company that works with leaders of various arms of government, NGOs and religious institutions as well as business and institutional leaders at all levels, using home-grown research and principle-based methodologies.

He also shepherds towering net-worth individuals, HIGH-PROFILE companies and institutions. He is also an outstanding columnist, thought leader, an exemplary author of ten books and a much-in-demand conference speaker in Nigeria and beyond.

11

SOCIAL RESPONSIBILITY:

THE NEW NORMAL FOR SOLIDARITY

Mar Introini

This chapter discusses the role of social responsibility in creating solidarity. Many people resist the idea of looking at COVID-19 as an opportunity rather than a devastating reality that we must get rid of as soon as possible. However, we would be a short-minded if we solely focus on the negative impacts rather than heralding the beginning of a new way of living and a renewed sense of preserving nature and lives. The importance of giving becomes vividly apparent in times of crisis such as this pandemic. Solidarity and empathy for others' pain cannot be viewed as a matter of exchange or immediate reward, but rather as an 'act & forget' exercise of small acts that finally leads into a massive wave of international solidarity.

In this vein, Burger King UK recently extended a goodwill gesture by encouraging customers to order from its competitors, thereby engaging in business as a fair game and not a war and vindicating the capacity to gain without undermining others' work. For the sake of improving the current poor conditions of the business sector and boost employment, they are building a new sense of doing business without prejudice, innovating and trailblazing a new culture based on trust, confidence, and resilience. Burger King UK has established new parameters that demand a sense of solidarity and empathy without losing focus on profits and competitive standing. We need more of such acts of kindness and generosity that transcend diverse political ideologies or business competitors, including individuals struggling to tackle COVID-19 from different approaches.

Unfortunately, when business competitors turn their action into aggression and political leaders become locked in endless contestation, we face the cruel reality of a 'blind path' towards the loss of resilience at the personal or partisan levels. In these cases, there is no sense of "giving" but only 'receiving' profits, votes, or power. The absence of a correct synergy among actors tends to sink a society into stagnation, thereby making good policies ineffective due to a lack of implementation that engages all actors, institutions, and leaders from a social rather than political focus. The creation of cohesion starts with a system built on structured solidarity, which is impossible when politicians become diverted by self-interest. However, the pandemic has shown us the massive social benefits that can be gained by forming innovative partnerships whereby creative leadership comes from diverse sources to foster social resilience. We are coming to realize the importance of acting from a point of social responsibility; rather than the traditional, failing model of political-institutional authority, we must shape a new paradigm that embraces joint action by all actors. Accepting a new normal means also accepting new rules and pushing for change at the systemic level.

Key words: Social responsibility, COVID 19, Creative leadership.

BIOGRAPHY

Mar Introini

Mar Introini PhD is a blogger, political analyst, trainer, facilitator, writer, and speaker with a legal background as a former Public Attorney. She has a strong sense of independent thinking and free learning on a continuous basis and a wide experience in living in different cities with diverse cultures (Montevideo, London, Brussels, Geneva, Malaga, Madrid) that helped on the road to build a spirit around multiculturalism and a versatile professional profile. Currently her focus is on developing a reshaped model of globalization, addressing several aspects of this "multiple crisis" state of the planet. A holistic approach seems to be the only way to build resilience in the short term and it is for that reason that she addresses a wide range of aspects around sustainability from a political perspective.

* * "Solidarity beyond charity" To contact Mar Introini https://thesustainabilityreader.com/2019/12/30/solidarity-beyond-charity/

12

UNTAPPED OPPORTUNITIES IN AFRICA

Olajide Abiola

My faith in the continent of Africa stems from a strong conviction that is nurtured by knowledge of the continent's truest possibilities. These bright potentials have motivated Western adventurers to invade the continent in droves to exploit its untapped and underdeveloped opportunities. As a developing continent, Africa presents enormous possibilities that are grossly lacking in the world's developed continents and nations. The broad lack of development on the continent presents more intervention and venture opportunities than any other continent for an array of aspiring young minds across diverse fields. There are areas of social progress to be pursued, social and business enterprises to be built, laws and policies to be enacted and passed, and industries to be developed from scratch; all of which represent a multitude of openings and the added benefit of getting things right or even better by observing the progress and success of other nations and continents.

Many young Africans have an erroneous impression about migration to Western nations. They feel that a developed society represents everything that is lacking on the African continent. Most literally associate development with opportunities—hence the desire to leave a country like Nigeria rather than contributing towards its national and economic development. They wrongly assume that the West's general socio-economic and socio-political development and stability translate into an axiomatic easier and better life than what the African continent offers. This misperception is largely fuelled by ignorance and a shallow view of the world and the multi-dimensional intricacies of a socially and economically advanced West to which they must spend many years adjusting before they can achieve a modicum of integration with their new environment, which can be a very daunting experience.

Untapped business ideas are ventures that no one considers to be potentially profitable. It may require a lot of financial investment or even stable electricity to keep such a business afloat. Generating ideas may take some time, and the process begins with exploring loopholes and filling the gaps so you can bring into existence that which did not previously exist. We have foreigners from different parts of the world investing in various bonds and stock investments, bank investments and real estate invents to mention a few.

In the words of Kofi Anan, "Africa's profitability is one of the best-kept secrets." We perceive this to indeed be true to the last word; Africa's potential is not only hidden from the outside world but also remains obscured to Africans themselves.

Africa's potential as a growth market for business remains both underestimated and misunderstood—as does the possibility for business to play a transformative role in solving the continent's biggest challenges. The drive to ensure that Africa reaps its reward in business innovation and investment is challenging but not impossible. Achieving this goal entails using Africa's manifold resources to the continent's advantage, and this is where the issue of population comes into play. Africa's current population is about 1.2 billion people, and it is projected to reach 1.7 billion by 2030. More than 80 percent of Africa's population growth over the next few decades will occur in cities, making it the fastest-urbanizing region in the world. At the same time, incomes are rising across much of the continent, generating new business opportunities in the consumer market. It is envisaged that if this situation continues to remain stable, then annual spending by African consumers and businesses could reach $6.66 trillion by 2030, up from $4 trillion in 2015.

Some sectors have increased their economic relevance by greater margins than others. In this regard, a comparison between the tourism, infrastructure, communication, health, and education sectors might bolster the negative perception being sold to the world that Africa is not development-oriented. There are opportunities in Nigeria: in 2018, Airbnb reported that the Nigerian market is attracting a growing number of tourists. For example, a company known as Gidanka signs long-term leases with apartment owners and then rents them out to businesspeople and leisure seekers as short-term lodging. In terms of youth employment, recruiters have expressed disappointment that approximately 50% of Nigerian graduates who are job seekers lack necessary skills for the workplace. It is obvious that there is a need for trainers to help these youths meet standards. The pandemic has created opportunities to use online assessments and training, which would reduce the cost of travelling so that anyone can access these opportunities regardless of their location.

SUMMARY

In summary, many Africans have left the continent for greener pastures; however, they end up being caught in a system that was not built with them in mind. The Western nations to which many are traveling already have their own procedures and structures, which are more advanced than in African countries. In contrast, there are untapped opportunities for entrepreneurs ready to solve problems and innovate to meet Africa's unmet needs. Regardless of the obstacles that we face, there is tremendous opportunity for growth that remains attractive to foreign investors.

BIOGRAPHY

Olajide Abiola

Olajide Abiola is a Military Veteran with a B.Sc in Computer Science from the University of Ilorin. prior to venturing into entrepreneurship and building structured businesses, he was a Regional Manager for ConSol, one of Nigeria's leading BPO. Prior to this role, he was an Identity Solutions consultant, selling software and hardware products and services across a broad spectrum of industries and sectors and even consulting for multinationals. He is the co-founder and CEO of KiaKia, one of Nigeria's pioneering Fintech's focused on digital lending, credit scoring and Peer to Peer on-lending which was launched in 2016 and has facilitated over N9bn in consumer and MSMEs loan disbursements in the last 6 years of operations. KiaKia is the recipients of several industry awards and recognitions.

Olajide is also the co-founder and CEO of Gidanka, a real estate and hospitality service provider that develops and designs upper upscale living spaces in fantastic neighbourhoods across the Abuja Cityscape, with presence in Jabi, Katampe Extension, Maitama, Asokoro, Wuye. Olajide Abiola is the founder and CEO of wheat Genius Limited, the Producers of the NAFDAC approved Krizpi KuliKuli, which is widely distributed across Nigeria and for exports. He is the founder of Jendo Oil Limited, the producers of premium pure and refined groundnut Oil in 4 sizes. He is also the co-founder of a Mill that produces primary and secondary raw materials for local industries and multinationals. The company also trades commodities as a major trade partner to many multinationals within the Agro-allied space. He the Founder and CEO of Jendo Kitchen trading as TheCityKitchen. A chain of fast-growing restaurant in the City of Abuja. His companies presently employ over 200 persons directly and about 43 indirectly. Olajide is Married with two kids.

13

THE IMPACT OF DIGITAL TRANSFORMATION ON ECONOMIC GROWTH

Akintola Akinsanya

ABSTRACT

This chapter examines the impact of digital transformation on economic growth in Africa and its significance for educational systems on the continent. The digital internet age is presenting major opportunities in the development space in the 21st century. Technology is disrupting the status quo in every single sector, with impacts ranging from financial access to property rights, health to education, and energy to water as well as government services, outcome measurements, implementation methods, and ways to connect to stakeholders like never before. For the first time in human history, we can theoretically connect to every single stakeholder, and technology can exponentially facilitate the achievement of development goals and potentially provide dividends for the world's poorest people (Schiller, 2016). In Africa, digital transformation has been instrumental to rapid expansions in telecommunications accessibility, economic growth, job creation in key sectors and societal awareness. In *fact, digital technology has become an integral part of daily life and a game changer among the general population and college/ university students. However, the talent and energy of Africa's young people is being poorly served by many of its underperforming education systems. Across low-income countries, only eight percent of children are on track to master basic secondary education-level skills in areas such as math, language arts, and critical thinking (ICFGEO, 2016), the latter of which is especially needed for digital creativity and exploration. Moving forward, the impacts of digital transformation have changed the face of economic growth and industrialization, human capital enhancement, and poverty alleviation to some extent and increased opportunities for youth. If all necessary conditions and disciplines are satisfied, the long-term positive effects of digital transformation will overshadow its preconceived negative effects.*

PURPOSE

African organizations are currently experiencing a rapid shift in the ways they harness digital transformation, and it is important for organizations to join this trend and understand how to profit from it.

METHODOLOGY/APPROACH

Investigative approach in businesses within cities and outside cities using Nigeria as a point of focus.

KEYWORDS

Invention, digital media, economic growth.

The current era has been described as 'the Information Age', a period characterised by the increasing use of digital technology to mediate access to and management of information (Mason, 1989; Castells, 2010). Therefore, the continent's progress among the comity of nations hinges on the value she places on digital media. Digital communication has many forms, including, inter alia, mobile phones, email, artificial intelligence and voice-enabled technology, and it has revolutionized our ability to transcend limits imposed by time and space. For example, the telephone has come a long way since its invention by Alexander Graham Bell in 1876. Telephones previously relied on landlines to send signals across the world and later made use of undersea cables. The first mobile phone was invented in 1973, and the first cell phone call was made by Dr Martin Cooper of Motorola to his rival at Bell Labs (Shiels, 2003). Since then, phones have come to enable much more than vocal communication, using tower and satellite signals to send text messages and data such as video and images.

Computers are the centrepiece of information technology. The early 1990s saw the emergence of household internet use, which eventually spurred the common usage of email, websites, blogs, social networking, video chat and voice-over-internet-protocol. Today, computers are critical for communication, and traditional communication modes such as postal mail and landline phones seem obsolete (Victor, n.d.).

Let's take a look at a few statistics. Africa has experienced an exponential growth of internet users over the last two decades, ranging from 367% in Reunion to 3.72 million percent in Democratic Republic of the Congo from 2000–2021 (Internet World Stats, 2021). It is estimated that over 100 million people across Africa were using Facebook monthly in 2014, and over 80% of such usage occurred via mobile (Constine, 2014)). Since, then, the number of African Facebook subscribers has skyrocketed to over 255 million people, including over 10 million in Kenya, over 24 million in South Africa, and over 31 million in Nigeria (Internet World Stats, 2021).

According to Mitchell (2015), Africa is also enjoying a booming e-commerce sector for those using computers and phones with mobile broadband access. Nigeria's answer to Amazon, Jumia, provides an entry route for international brands wanting to enter the African market. Moreover, money transfer transactions are proliferating across the continent. For example, MPesa enables individuals in Kenya to deposit, withdraw and transfer money as well as pay for goods and services using their mobile phones. In most urbanized areas, local ride-sharing services such as Little Cab in Kenya, Jrney in South Africa, and Pickmeup in Nigeria as well as international competitors such as Uber and China's DiDi Chuxing also enable people to easily obtain taxi rides and pay their fares using mobile wallet apps (Cheng, 2021; Mourdoukoutas, 2017).

When the Millennium Development Goals (MDGs) were

ratified in 2000, there was no such thing as Facebook, iPhone, Twitter, etc. However, today, smartphones and social media have become indispensable and powerful tools for inclusive sustainable development, and it is practically impossible to imagine devising solutions to the myriad problems of today and the future without them.

William Churchill's statement, 'Never let crisis go to waste', vividly sums up the proliferation of innovations in Africa during the coronavirus pandemic. Among other challenges, most African countries experienced difficulties accessing expensive technology-based solutions to combat the pandemic, local individuals and companies began developing their own innovative products. For example, in Nigeria, a user-friendly app called Wellvis was built to provide on-demand self-assessments of individuals' coronavirus risk category based on their symptoms and exposure history, a Ghanaian team developed a tool to map and classify test cases according to risk and submit the data to national authorities, and in Uganda, a university professor collaborated with a car manufacturer Kiira Motors to produce affordable ventilators to supply the country's health care system (Nebe and Jalloh, 2020). App-based food delivery services to support social distancing include the Zimbabwean Fresh In A Box and the Ugandan Market Garden app (Nebe and Jalloh, 2020).

It is my submission that internet use, mobile money transfers, digital apps and mobile apps are all contributing to economic growth in Africa. Although the global coronavirus pandemic has slowed growth on the continent much as it has done worldwide, African innovators remain undaunted and continue to explore new solutions to ensure the region's survival while also enhancing its prosperity.

REFERENCES

Castells, M. (2010). *The rise of the network society: The information age: economy, society, and culture*. Chichester: Wiley.

Cheng, M. (2021). Uber drivers in Africa are taking notes from their triumphant British peers. *Africa Quartz*, 18 April. https://qz.com/africa/1997485/africa-uber-drivers-take-note-of-wins-by-uk-drivers/

Constine, J. (2014). Facebook hits 100m users in Africa, half the continent's internet-connected population. *techcrunch*, 08 September. https://techcrunch.com/2014/09/08/facebook-africa/

Internet World Stats (2021). Africa internet usage, 2021 population stats and Facebook subscribers. https://www.internetworldstats.com/stats1.htm

Jensen, J. (1988). Using the typewriter: secretaries, reporters, authors, 1880-1930. *Technology in Society*, 10, 255-266.

Mason, R.O. (1986). Four ethical issues of the information age. *Management Information Systems Quarterly, 10,* 5-12.

Mitchell, P. (2015). *How digital is unleashing Africa's creativity?* Retrieved from www.weforum.org

Nebe, C. and Jalloh, A.-B. (2020). Coronavirus pandemic driving tech solutions in sub-Saharan Africa. *DW*, 19 April. https://www.dw.com/en/coronavirus-pandemic-driving-tech-solutions-in-sub-saharan-africa/a-53175841

Schiller, B. (2016). How the technology behind Bitcoin is going to change the lives of the bottom billion. *Fast Company.* https://www.fastcompany.com/3056481/how-the technology-behind-bitcoin-is-going-to-change-the-lives-of-the-bottom-billion

Shiels, M. 2003). *A chat with the man behind mobiles*. BBC News, 21 April. http://news.bbc.co.uk/2/hi/uk_news/2963619.stm

Victor, J. (n.d.). The importance of computers in communication. *Techwalla.* https://www.techwalla.com/articles/the-importance-of-computers-in-communication

BIOGRAPHY

Akintola Akinsanya

Akintola Akinsanya is a Sales and Customer Acquisition Professional with over 15 years of experience in sales. Akintola is a public speaker, author, political analyst, and business advisor who combine his experience of global savvy and creativity ingenuity with his intuitive understanding of people and events. Akintola earned a degree in Political Science from Olabisi Onabanjo University back in 2013/14. Akintola is a Principal Partner at Be Empowered Global Business – a no-guesswork Sales, Training, Supplies and General Contract Resource Company based in Lagos, Nigeria. He's the convener of Be Empowered Book Club and The Mentoring Mind Network.

Also, he once writes for iShine Magazine, a UK-based magazine which specializes in publishing the achievements of Africans (especially Nigerians) both in print and online for a global audience. Akintola is also an ambassador for The Nous Organisation Incorporated, An organisation that share, educate and inform on various issues around mental health. One of his co-authored works "Mediterranean Odysseus: A Political Economy Outlook on Roles of Afro-European Relations to Africa Mass Migration in the 21st Century and the Broad Effects" appeared in International Journal of Humanities and Social Sciences. His long term goal is to become a national-regional-international level policy, politics, and governance adviser. He wants to use his indefatigable commitment and drive to bring more dignity to the people across the world. Akintola had a lot of significant professional experiences as a Sales and Customer Acquisition Professional. He recently bagged a Business and Entrepreneurship Certification at the Joseph Business School, Lagos with the headquarter located in Forest Park, Illinois, USA.

14

YOUTH IDENTITY

AND THE CHALLENGES

Olivia B. J-Olajide-Aluko

INTRODUCTION

The global population of young people between the ages of 10 and 24 is currently over 1.8 billion and is the fastest-growing of all age groups (United Nations Population Fund, 2014). These groups of people experience unique challenges, some of which are less easily recognised and generally hidden, whereas others are more glaring and can be addressed by government parastatals. Young people are growing up faster than in previous decades and are becoming more aware of both the positive and negative issues that surround them. A central theme encountered when listening to different youths is that they 'do not just want to be a statistic'; they want a place where they belong. They want to be a part of the decision process that concerns them.

From their teens, youths become more conscious of their body image and appearance. A parent may have to remind their 10–

12 year-old child to bathe and groom themselves; however, by the time that child has become a fully-fledged teen at 15 years old, the parent will find them fully engaged in such behaviours. If your child is teen boy, you may wake up one morning and find out that your socks are suddenly disappearing, and if she is a girl, she is starting to use some of your make up. It is during this period that all the flaws that the youths never saw in their bodies—from birthmarks to the shape of their nose or teeth—suddenly start to become problematic.

One cannot rule out the impact of social media on today's youths, particularly with regard to their body image. Filled with images of 'perfect' people with flawless skin and perfect body shapes and hair, social media have redefined body image among youths, many of whom are unduly influenced to idolise celebrities and other icons. Thus, some youths are pushed to imitate what they see as 'perfection', thereby endangering their lives and developing eating disorders, whereas others become so obsessed with narcissistic behaviours such as taking selfie pictures or other forms of self-promotion.

Youths also face the pressure of materialism, which distorts their attitude toward money and distracts them from proper investment of their resources. It is common for youths to look for easy ways to make money that do not require education or hard work. Perhaps this accounts for why so many Black males in the western world are prone to engage in 'drug dealing' to make quick money.

Some youths also have problems at home; if they are struggling to find love and support among their family, there is the tendency for them to seek it outside among their peers. Youths also reach a stage in their lives when they want to explore; they may prefer to look to their peers for solutions rather than to listen to instructions from parents and other well-meaning elders.

Youths experience varying challenges; however, the quest to succeed in education and employment is of paramount concern on a global scale. Regardless of where youths are around the world, it is obvious that economic recessions impact revenue and job availability, which often has corresponding impacts on youth employment. One of the major challenges facing the world today is the growing decline of permanent careers or employment. Multiple variables have impacted today's job market, and careers that were thriving in the 1990s have now become obsolete; thus, it is possible to be forced to change careers 2–4 times over the course of one's working life.

Many of the world's developed countries have witnessed unprecedented changes in recent decades, as workforces have shifted from being dominated by manufacturing, discrete skill requirements, and an expectation of a long tenure with a single company to constantly evolving labour markets in which companies expect transferable skills and workers must constantly anticipate job changes. This has a significant impact on students and new graduates, and many young people's hopes are being dashed as a consequence of these massive economic changes. Having secured their education with loans, the average young person graduates from university steeped in debt, and then they struggle to find jobs that provide a living wage. Some graduates even discover that they need to change their career paths, due either to a lack of available jobs in their field of study or a lack of experience and companies' willingness to risk giving them the opportunity to gain the experience they need.

Whereas some differences in youth quality of life can be attributed to living in wealthier or poorer nations, experiences vary even among young people in the developed world, as there are different privileges open to those who obtain their education at community or lower ranked colleges and those are able to attend prestigious institutions such as the UK Russell Group of universities or the US Ivy League universities. Whereas the latter often already have jobs waiting for them upon graduation, those from average working class or poor backgrounds, and particularly many members of Black and Minority ethnic groups repeatedly find themselves having to prove their worth either through their academic scores or ingenuity.

A 2016 report by the UK Equality and Human Rights Commission (EHRC, 2016) revealed that Black African and Caribbean men faced 'systemic barriers' hindering their ability to enter elite UK universities, including discriminatory entry processes, low numbers of ethnic minority staff, and uneven awarding of qualifications. Only 6% of Black secondary school graduates attend one of the 24 leading UK universities, compared with 11 percent of white school leavers (EHRC, 2015).

A 2015 survey reported in *The Guardian* reported an approximately 49% rise in the number of 16- to 24-year-olds from ethnic minority communities who were long-term unemployed over the past five years, even while unemployment among young white people fell by 2% (Taylor, 2015). Overall, Black and minority youth are twice as likely to be unemployed than Whites (Francis-Devine and Foley, 2020). Moreover, significant pay disparities between black and white workers in the UK persist, with black workers earning more than 26 percent less than their white counterparts as of 2017 (Gangmasters and Labour Abuse Authority, 2017; Longhi and Brynin, 2017). According to the Trades Union Congress (TUC, 2016), Black workers with A-levels earn 14.3% less on average than their white counterparts, and even white workers who only have GSCEs earn more on average than black workers with A-levels. Black workers who leave school with GCSEs typically get paid 11.4% less than their white peers, and those with higher education degrees earn 23.1% less on average than white workers with degrees (TUC, 2016). As a result, significant numbers of black workers in the UK live in poverty; 28% and 31% of men and women of black African descent, respectively, do not earn a living wage, as well as 19% and 20% of men and women of black Caribbean descent, respectively (Longhi and Brynin, 2017).

Recent figures demonstrate similar race-based pay gaps in the United States, which have steadily increased over the past 20 years. Overall, in 2018, Black workers earned 27.5% less than White workers compared with 21.8% in 2000; those with high school or college degrees earned 21% less than their counterparts compared with 15.3% and 17.2% in 2000, respectively, and those with advanced degrees earned 18.5% less compared with 12.5% less in 2000 (Gould, 2019). The pay gap between African-American and White workers in the highest paid professions is a staggering 33.4% (Gould, 2019).

PREPARING YOUTH FOR THE FUTURE

The above-described trends paint a stark picture for youth of African descent and an urgent need to better prepare them for the future. Achieving that goal requires that the issues faced by youth be transformed into opportunities. A major positive dimension of the economic transformation in developed countries is that ongoing growth continues to change the way business is done, and new developments in financial practices, sciences, technology, and artificial intelligence are opening up new jobs and directions for youths. On the one hand, many jobs now require more than a high school diploma; however, those who educate themselves in preparation for entering this market will gain access to higher paying work that will enable them to thrive. Moreover, the globalisation of the world economy and related technological advances have the door to fruitful entrepreneurship opportunities that will enable motivated youth to use their ingenuity to prosper independently. Being aware of such opportunities will enable us to prepare young people to take advantage of them.

Youths are largely full of life and energy; however, these qualities can easily be misdirected if they do not have a vision for what they want to achieve in life. Youths need direction and focus. For example, a lack of vision can lead youths to choose fields careers that are not ideal for them without truly understand why they are pursuing that line of study, and they become further confused as they enter into the world of work, as they are not finding fulfilment in the fields they have pursued.

Education for the future must include soft skills such as verbal communication, social awareness, emotional intelligence, problem solving, and planning for success. Other complementary or generic skills include interpersonal communication, negotiation skills, the ability to clearly present ideas, and teamwork skills. Personal values can make a difference in a work setting or across an enterprise and are proven to influence the way in which decisions are made. A lot of people can earn a diploma or a degree; however, the most valuable features of strong job candidates are not taught but rather are intrinsic. For example, 'having a positive attitude' is a vital skill. A negative attitude is a drain upon the hearers; youths with an 'I can do' mentality will always find opportunities for development and growth. Moreover, a capacity for critical thinking and independent thought is vital; living as a 'copycat' who is ruled by others' ideas limits the ability to determine one's own ambitions and constrains the opportunities that are available to young people.

EXPLORING YOUTH MIGRATION IN AFRICA

According to a report released by the African Union (2020), Africa has more than 400 million young people between the ages of 15 and 35 years, which accounts for 70% of the continent's population. The youth population aged 15–24 in Africa is projected to double from 231 million to 461 million by 2050 (United Nations Conference on Trade and Development, 2018).

The African continent is the worst-hit region when youth challenges are brought to light. Much of Africa's regional and international migration is closely related to the massive growth in the youth population, which is occurring at a faster rate than any place in the world. Many youths are choosing migration as a means to pursue true adulthood through education and employment. If one asks a group of average youth in Africa how many of them want to travel abroad, many will answer affirmatively. However, more probing questions regarding why they wish to leave or what they want to do often receive vague responses: most simply say they 'just to go and work', 'just any work'.

An obvious outgrowth of low and vulnerable employment, poverty is a central cause the need for the youth to migrate to other global regions. In the recent past, there are basic needs that have been regarded as a luxury, such as eating two meals a day (Mago, 2018). Youth perceive that it will be easier for them to improve their lives better or access employment opportunities. It is common for youths in African countries to want to migrate, as many believe that they are safe and immune from their challenges once they leave their host country. Consequently, some of these youths have risked their lives by journeying through the Mediterranean Sea to come to Europe, whereas others have fallen into the hands of smugglers and slave traders who have promised them that there are jobs waiting for them upon arrival in their country of destination. Not all youths leave Africa as a matter of choice, some are forced into situations where fleeing their countries of origin are the only viable options. However, migration is not a simple endeavour. Those who migrate as students and economic migrants experience different struggles depending on their characteristics and disposable income and class; however, across cases, there are hurdles to overcome in order to achieve labour market or social integration. The migration of youth to other parts of the world may individually be perceived as a positive move; however, it may prove disastrous for some, who they find themselves in menial jobs despite their qualifications.

Multiple factors contribute to youth migration in Africa (Chinyakata and Raselekoane, 2018). The unavailability of employment opportunities not only renders the youth jobless but also increases their chances of deciding to leave their regions to seek employment opportunities in other parts of the world, where they believe there are still more opportunities for employment (Dwyer, and Wyn, 2004). A major challenge for African youths is finding and securing good jobs in their home countries. Amid long-stagnating job markets, 50–90% of the total labour force in West and Central Africa is either unemployed or working unstable jobs, and young people have 20% lower employment rates than adults (AFDB, 2018). Job scarcity and instability have resulted in increasing numbers of youth emigrating for job opportunities. Africa is ranked as the leader of the importer of professional expertise to other parts of the world, as the continent's governments are not able to absorb the professionals.

However, even as migration is often driven by the lack of employment opportunities, it may also emerge as a response to the challenges posed by the growing populations of unemployed youth. Young people are generally boisterous, talented, creative, technologically adept and ambitious, and often like to experiment with new ideas. Consequently, it is much easier for them to be adventurous towards relocating out of their familiar surroundings. However, youth must be made to understand that education will open more windows for creativity and talent for income. Above all, they have to be made aware of the importance of finding income-generating activities that will enable them to meet their daily expenses and improve their economic status.

AFRICAN EDUCATIONAL SYSTEMS AND YOUTH
UNEMPLOYMENT

In addition to other structural deficiencies, poverty in Africa is a result of poor educational systems (Moalusi, 2018). African schools do not equip learners with the skills and expertise to be self-reliant and practical; rather, education is largely knowledge-based at both the lower and higher levels, and students are merely equipped with theories with no clue to practically implement the skills learned. It appears that African regimes of the 21st century are still in the business of equipping people with theoretical knowledge without considering the practicability of that knowledge in the market where the expertise can be of importance. However, the African education system is no longer market-friendly and therefore does not meet employers' needs. The system was designed for an obsolete time of low unemployment rates and high human resource demand, and entrepreneurial activities were limited and generally non-lucrative. From a young age, people have been informed to work hard in school to be employed by reputable organizations (Wossen and Ayele, 2018), and if one does not secure employment, it is taken to mean that they did not score sufficiently high grades to qualify for hiring. Hence, even today, despite the radical changes in the labour market, the young person who has failed to obtain employment is regarded as a disgrace and unwanted element in society.

As more emphasis is placed on solving the global youth unemployment menace, it is important to deal with the factors that contribute to the phenomenon (Mpungose and Monyae, 2018). For one, as much as employment has been an issue in the world, the term has often been mis-conceptualised. Society tends to believe that employment comes with a two-way traffic system in which fresh graduates be attached to a given organization in order to earn income or make a living (Choung and Manamela, 2018). There is a misperception that employment is based on hiring someone's services for an income return. The system has created experts who are dependent on trading their services for wages; however, the growing problem of unemployment should be an indicator of the fact that the demand has shifted to another level altogether.

One problem that has been long overlooked in the economic environment is that most of the academically qualified youth in Africa lack employment opportunities in their areas of training and expertise. In order to improve the youth outlook, it is imperative to overhaul the educational system world to open the way for entrepreneurial motivation and spirit (Gukurume, 2018), which will enable young graduates to both employ themselves and create jobs for other unemployed youth. The education offered to African youth must to be adapted to suit the ever-changing job market (Akanle and Omotayo, 2019), in which working can also comprise self-employment and entrepreneurship (Assan and Nalutaaya,

2018). The educational system must be based on a curriculum that enables the unemployed to innovate and eventually employ themselves (Yami et al., 2019). Governments and their agents should constantly review their curricula to align youth education and training with industry and market needs.

In today's global economy, certain types of skills determine whether young people will be able to find work, contribute to their local and national economies, and live up to their individual developmental and earning potentials. In addition to foundation skills, or basic literacy and numeracy skills, and technical and vocational skills, it is also critical to master soft skills, also known as transferrable skills, such as analysis, communication, problem solving, creativity, and leadership, which can be transferred and adapted across different environments. These sorts of skills are usually learned in the western world through schools or other support services for training. However, as detailed above, in many African countries, emphasis is placed on education within school walls and the accumulation of degrees; thus, a person may earn two to three master's degrees but lack the emotional intelligence or problem solving and conflict resolution skills to maintain a job.

As a part of transforming education, changing the notions, mental formations, and expectations of young intellectuals is a paramount yet complex task. Young upcoming professionals should not be mentally fed with a delivery of a job once done with their school or career; rather, they have to be prepared to improve their economic status through innovations and entrepreneurship skills. Youth have to be told point-blank that education in terms of theories may not improve their living standards, as the world has metamorphosised to a point at which no level of education can guarantee a better life; rather, it is the level of skills and experience that matters today. The marketability of an individual in the current economic set-up depends on the uniqueness of their experience and skillset to develop innovative products and services or devise solutions to verifiable problems (Achinewhu-Nworgu, 2019). This is what youth have to be informed before they delve into any career.

REFORMING THE SOCIAL-POLITICAL ENVIRONMENT

Being a youth in Africa is not about age alone. Adulthood is first and foremost defined in social and economic terms as well as by marriage, parenthood, and a family livelihood. In this context, millions of young adult Africans find themselves *stagnating in their youth* well beyond the age of 25 in what Vigh described as 'a predicament of not being able to gain the status and responsibility of adulthood [...] a social position that people seek to escape as it is characterized by marginality, stagnation, and a truncation of social being' (2006, p. 37). During this indefinite period between childhood and adulthood, young people cannot expect assistance from either their parents or the state but do not yet enjoy the full social and legal privileges of adulthood (Honwana, 2012).

How can African youth respond to their social stagnation and the denial of their adulthood, particularly in an environment that limits political mobilisation? The governance in African countries has not prioritised ethics, power-sharing or free speech; rather, corruption, public untruthfulness and the stifling of opposition are all too common among the leadership in African countries. Particularly, the individualism in leadership is a core wound that has made youth challenges of any version to reciprocate. These forces give rise to new challenges that make youth endangered individuals in the modern world (Buganga, 2018).

In Africa as well as globally, youth have never been allowed to express their potential in governance, as they are believed to have lack wisdom and experience and insufficiently value their culture (Mueller et al 2018). Therefore, youth are not provided with an enabling environment with their respective authorities. Feeling ignored and neglected, the only means to air their views is through protests and street demonstrations, which are characterised by elders and leaders as signs of hate and disrespect. Hence, African youths' demands for employment opportunities are translated as a rebellion against their culture influenced by the westernized way of life relayed to them by the media. However, 21st century African youths' openness to external cultural forces can also be seen as evidence of their dynamism and adaptability for survival in a rapidly changing world. Rather than viewing this flexibility as a sign of cultural deterioration, it is critical to reform education in a manner that can guide their process of development and realignment by formulating positive ways to maintain their culture in their day-to-day lives.

CONCLUSION

Investing in youth by providing education, health care, and job opportunities is imperative if national governments seek to reduce poverty and diminish urban drift and brain drain from migration. Policies and programs must recognise youth, and decision-makers need to engage them in formulating and implementing poverty reduction strategies. With this framework, youth can improve their livelihoods through self-sustaining employment prospects, education, health care, and social life. Young Africans need access to marketable education and opportunities to acquire vocational and life skills to actively participate in all spheres of an increasingly knowledge-intensive society. Unfortunately, too young people in Africa struggle to acquire an education that provides them with employable skills and knowledge. As a result, the transition from school-to-work is a major challenge, and many young Africans end up either unemployed or vulnerably employed in the informal sector with limited prospects or security.

As the links between migration, brain drain, and youth unemployment have become increasingly clear, governments and international organisations have focused significant efforts to improve this situation in recent years. The private sector and non-profit organizations can also contribute to this endeavour for example, many African countries have directed resources and efforts toward universal primary school enrolment, and the number of vocational and technical schools is growing. Public-private partnerships can both help overcome limitations in the education sector through providing training and assisting in curriculum development to help fill the gaps between formal education and the labour market.

REFERENCES

African Union. Youth development. Retrieved from https://au.int/en/youth-development

Altman, M., 2007. Youth labour market challenges in South Africa. Human Sciences Research Council. Retrieved from https://miriamaltman.com/wp-content/uploads/2016/09/LAB_MKT035_Altman_Youth_lbr_mkt_challenges.pdf

Ajufo, B.I., 2013. Challenges of youth unemployment in Nigeria: Effective career guidance as a panacea. *African Research Review*, *7* (1), pp.307-321.

Akanle, O. and Omotayo, A., 2019. Youth, unemployment and incubation hubs in Southwest Nigeria. *African Journal of Science, Technology, Innovation and Development*, pp.1-8.

Anna, B. and Eva, B., 2018. Beyond cultural racism: Challenges for an anti-racist sexual education for youth. In *Youth, Sexuality and Sexual Citizenship* (pp. 71-85). Routledge.

Assan, J.K. and Nalutaaya, V.H., 2018. Africa's youth unemployment challenge and the pursuit of soft skills development by university students. *Review of European Studies*, *10*(3).

Buganga, J.W., 2018. African Buddhist perspectives on challenges and opportunities in youth participation in good governance and peace building. *The Journal of International Association of Buddhist Universities (JIABU)*, *11*(3), pp.432-441.

Chinyakata, R. and Raselekoane, R.N., 2018. A study of the effects of Zimbabwean youth migration on Musina Area, South Africa. *The Social Sciences*, *13*(2), pp.357-362.

Choung, M.E. and Manamela, M.G., 2018. Digital inequality in rural and urban settings: challenges of education and information in South African youth context. *Bangladesh e-Journal of Sociology*, *15*(2).

Derenne, J. and Beresin, E., 2018. Body image, media, and eating disorders—a 10-year update. *Academic Psychiatry*, *42*(1), pp.129-134.

Durham, D., 2000. Youth and the social imagination in Africa: Introduction to parts 1 and 2. *Anthropological quarterly*, *73*(3), pp.113-120.

Dwyer, P. and Wyn, J., 2004. *Youth, education and risk: Facing the future*. Routledge.

Equality and Human Rights Commission, 2015. *Is Britain fairer? The state of equality and human rights 2015*. Retrieved from https://www.equalityhumanrights.com/sites/default/files/is-britain-fairer-2015.pdf

Equality and Human Rights Commission, 2016. Healing a divided Britain: the need for a comprehensive race equality strategy. Retrieved from https://www.equalityhumanrights.com/sites/default/files/healing_a_divided_britain_-_accessible_version_-_final.docx

Francis-Devine, B., and Foley, N., 2020. Unemployment by ethnic background. House of Commons Briefing Paper No. 6385. Retrieved from http://researchbriefings.files.parliament.uk/documents/ SN06385/SN06385.pdf

Gangmasters and Labour Abuse Authority, 2017. Ethnicity pay gap report 2017. Retrieved from https://www.london.gov.uk/sites/ default/files/gla-ethnicity-pay-gap-report-2017.pdf

Gjylbegaj, V., 2018. Media effects and body image perceptions on youth in UAE. *International E-Journal of Advances in Social Sciences*, 4(11), pp.415-423.

Gould, E., 2019. State of working America wages 2018: Wage inequality marches on—and is even threatening data reliability. Retrieved from https://www.epi.org/publication/state-of-american-wages-2018/

Gukurume, S., 2018. *Strengthening small and medium enterprises to address youth unemployment crisis in Zimbabwe*. IDS Policy Briefing 154. Retrieved from https://www.ids.ac.uk/publications/ strengthening-small-and-medium-enterprises-to-address-youth-unemployment-crisis-in-zimbabwe/

Honwana, A. (2012). *The time of youth: work, social change, and politics in Africa*. West Hartford, CT: Kumarian Press.

Honwana, A., 2012. *The time of youth: work, social change, and politics in Africa*. West Hartford, CT: Kumarian Press.

Longhi, S. and Brynin, M., 2017. *Research report 108: the ethnicity pay gap*. Manchester: Equality and Human Rights Commission. Retrieved from: https://www.equalityhumanrights.com/en/our-research/list-all-our-research-reports

Mago, S., 2018. Urban youth unemployment in South Africa: socio-economic and political problems. *Commonwealth Youth and Development*, *16*(1), pp.1-16.

Matandare, M.A., 2018. Botswana unemployment rate trends by gender: Relative analysis with upper middle income Southern African countries (2000-2016). *Dutch Journal of Finance and Management*, *2*(2), p.04.

McCormick, M.H., 2009. The effectiveness of youth financial education: A review of the literature. *Journal of Financial Counseling and Planning*, *20*(1).

Moalusi, T., 2018. Youth unemployment in SA increasing-where to from here? *HR Future*, *2018*(Jul 2018), pp.8-9.

Motti-Stefanidi, F., 2018. Resilience among immigrant youth: The role of culture, development and acculturation. *Developmental Review*, *50*, pp.99-109.

Mpungose, L. and Monyae, L., 2018. *Carrying forward the momentum of the 2017 African Union Year of Youth*. Policy Insights 60, South African Institute of International Affairs. Retrieved from https://www.africaportal.org/publications/carrying-forward-momentum-2017-african-union-year-youth/

Mueller, V., Doss, C. and Quisumbing, A., 2018. Youth migration and labour constraints in African agrarian households. *The Journal of Development Studies*, *54*(5), pp.875-894.

Mugo, E.W. and Nyaegah, J.O., 2018. Role of information technology skills on youth empowerment projects: A case of

Nakuru Town, Kenya. *International Academic Journal of Information Sciences and Project Management*, *3*(2), pp.345-363.

Oluwatayo, I.B. and Ojo, A.O., 2018. Walking through a tightrope: The challenge of economic growth and poverty in Africa. *The Journal of Developing Areas*, *52*(1), pp.59-69.

Oti, A.R., 2019. Nollywood: popular culture and narratives of youth struggles in Nigeria. *African Studies Quarterly*, *18*(2), pp.129-130.

Taylor, M., 2015. 50% rise in long-term unemployment for young ethnic minority people in UK. *The Guardian,* 10 March. Retrieved fromhttps://www.theguardian.com/society/2015/mar/10/50-rise-in-long-term-unemployed-youngsters-from-uk-ethnic-minorities

Trades Union Congress, 2016. Black workers with degrees earn a quarter less than white counterparts, finds TUC. Retrieved from https://www.tuc.org.uk/news/black-workers-degrees-earn-quarter-less-white-counterparts-finds-tuc

United Nations Conference on Trade and Development, 2018. *Economic development in Africa report*. Retrieved from http://unctad.org/en/PublicationChapters/edar2018_ch1_en.pdf

United Nations Population Fund, 2014. *The power of 1.8 billion: adolescents, youth and the transformation of the future*. Retrieved from https://www.unfpa.org/sites/default/files/pub-pdf/EN-SWOP14-Report_FINAL-web.pdfWossen, T. and Ayele, S., 2018. Ethiopia's Agricultural Transformation: Agribusiness' Contribution to Reducing Youth Unemployment. *IDS Bulletin*, *49*(5).

Vigh, H. (2006). Navigating terrains of war: youth and soldiering in Guinea-Bissau. Oxford: Berghahn Books.

Yami, M., Feleke, S., Abdoulaye, T., Alene, A.D., Bamba, Z. and Manyong, V., 2019. African rural youth engagement in agribusiness: achievements, limitations, and lessons. *Sustainability*, *11*(1), p.185.

15

AFRICA'S YOUTH TRAILBLAZE IN COMMERCE AND INNOVATION (A FOCUS ON NIGERIA)

Adetunji Omotola

INTRODUCTION

Nineteen of the world's youngest nations are in Africa. However, approximately one-third of continent's 420 million youths aged 15–35 are unemployed. On the one hand, Africa's youth bulge coupled with massive youth unemployment is a ticking time bomb for the continent. On the other hand, there is ample evidence that Africa's youth are blazing trails in commerce, innovation, and agriculture.

PURPOSE

This essay highlights examples from countries like Nigeria, Zimbabwe, and South Africa to demonstrate that despite the high rate of unemployment among African youths, a growing number are contributing to the economy through commerce and innovation.

CONCLUSION

It was reported that on Sunday, the 15th of March   2021 in Abuja, Nigeria's capital, Dr. Ngozi Okonjo- Iweala, who was twice Nigeria's Finance Minister and a former Managing Director of the World Bank, made the following remarks: 'Nigeria has a lot of many young people with a lot of talent, our young people are on the internet producing and creating value, doing so many things in services, I was very heartened when President Muhammadu Buhari spoke about investing in young people'.

In his ringing endorsement of the prowess of African youths in the areas of commerce and innovation, Dr. Okonjo-Iweala, who is currently and the Director General of the World Trade Organization, singled out Flutterwave, a Nigerian fintech company valued at nearly $1 billion.

In the words of Olugbenga Agboola, Flutterwave's Chief Executive Officer, 'for Africa to leapfrog, we need to have three things, logistics, payments and commerce'. Flutterwave has built a common payment infrastructure that connects everything together and makes it easy for a business to accept payments either online or in-store. Recently signing a deal with PayPal to get back into the Nigerian market, the company is making huge strides in Nigeria and globally. Olugbenga noted that although Africa's payment types may be different and diverse, they are effective. Mobolaji Bammeke, Flutterwave's head of compliance and a former employee of JP Morgan, previously worked with teams from the US, UK and Europe to build businesses from the ground up. Since its founding in 2016, Flutterwave has built an enviable track record, accumulating a good book of blue-chip clients such as Safaricom and Airtel.

In the agriculture space, Alley Capital Group's Chief Executive Officer, Piwai Chikasha, and its Chief Operating Officer, Takudzwa Chapadza, are Zimbabweans specialising in supplying crop spraying services using advanced precision drones to farmers. Though both are from Zimbabwe, they started as strangers at an aeronautical engineering college in Ukraine. There, Piwai and Takudzwa developed their friendship as well as a mutual interest in development, which quickly turned into a business partnership. After graduating and moving back to their home country, they began toying with different project ideas in earnest. No idea was off the table. As they explained, 'We always had this idea of transferring all the knowledge we gained in Europe back to Zimbabwe.' They decided that the agricultural industry, with its ubiquitous, polluting diesel-powered tractors, was a valuable starting point, and they chose to primarily focus on small farmers. After extensive research and a thorough market analysis, Piwai and Takudzwa co-founded their smart agriculture and engineering company, Alley Capital Group.

Opeyemi Awoyemi (33), Ayodeji Adewunmi (37) and Olalekan Olude (37) founded Jobberman in their dormitory at Obafemi

Awolowo University, Nigeria to help connect people looking for jobs with companies that are hiring. According to Adewunmi, 'we were all students at that time and on the 9th of August 2009, I struck gold while reading the making of Naukri.com in the book *Stay Hungry, Stay Foolish* by Rashmi Bansal'. Jobberman.com is West Africa's most popular job search engine and aggregator. The service went live in August 2009, and it currently attracts over 50,000 unique users each day. Through simple but cutting -edge technology, Jobberman helps link qualified personnel to the right job opportunities. In 2011, Tiger Global became a Jobberman investor and by 2012, Jobberman was the single largest job placement website in sub-Saharan Africa. In February 2012, it was named number 8 in Forbes magazine Top 20 tech start-ups in Africa. In 2016, Facebook CEO Mark Zuckerberg cited Olude and others as examples of young Nigerians using digital technology to make impact across Africa.

Paystack, a Nigerian start-up company, was founded by Chief Executive Officer Shola Akinlade (34) and Chief Technology Officer Ezra Olubi (34). According to Akinlade, 'For us, it is about the mission. I am driven by the mission to accelerate payments on the continent, and I am convinced that Stripe will help us get there faster, it is a very natural move'. Stripe, a US company valued at $32 billion, acquired Paystack for $200 million in 2020.

Stripe had earlier led an $8 million funding round for Paystack, with other participants including Visa and Tencent. Like Stripe, Paystack provides a quick way to integrate payment services into online or offline transactions by way of an application programming interface (API). The company currently has around 60,000 customers, including small businesses, larger corporations, fintech companies, educational institutions, and online betting companies.

Apiwe Nxusani-Mawela (37) is the first black woman in South Africa to own a micro-brewery. Her company, Brewster's Craft, trains students in the science of beer making and provides quality testing services to professional breweries. Brewers Craft has a 1,000-litre contract manufacturing brewing facility, where it also offers laboratory services to other microbreweries. Brewster's Craft launched its own beer and cider brand, Tolokazi, in 2019. According to Nxusani-Mawela, 'our competitive advantage is that we use indigenous African ingredients in our beers and ciders'.

A major revolution is also evident in Africa's entertainment sector, led by the Nigerian trio of Burna Boy (29) Wizkid (30) and Davido (28), who are without doubt Africa's biggest three music stars. Master KG, (25), a South African, is another African music success story whose song 'Jerusalema' became a worldwide hit in 2020. The huge strides made by these artists are evident through collaborations with their counterparts in the United States, who have welcomed

Afrobeat and value the talent they bring. Burna Boy recently won a Grammy for the best African musician, and Wizkid won an award for featuring with Beyonce in the musical video 'Brown Skin Girl'. The YouTube views of these artists' official videos and their social media followings on Twitter and Instagram number into the millions. Master KG's 'Jerusalema' tops the log at 348 million, Burna Boy's 'On The Low' and Davido's 'Fall' have each racked up 198 million views, and Wizkid's 'Joro' has reached 107 million views.

It is patently clear that technology is a game changer for these young business superstars, and fintech is where they are finding big opportunities. Their businesses are scaling quickly, and they are attracting major investors from around the world. Africa's youths are on the move.

BIOGRAPHY

Adetunji Omotola

Adetunji Omotola BSc, MA, LLB, B.L is a Public Speaker, *Africa Enthusiast, and a journalist.* He holds a Masters in Communications research from the University of Leicester, an LLB Law from South Bank University London, and is a graduate of Sociology from the University of Lagos. His professional qualifications include Stockbroking, Certificate in Wine from the Cape Wine Academy and Certificates in Real Estate and Insurance from the UK and South Africa respectively. He is an alumnus of the Henley Business School Executive Speaker Programme. Adetunji is also a Bloomberg Media Certified Financial Journalist. He holds a certificate of attendance in Mandarin from The WITS Language School.

An African enthusiast dedicated to telling the African story across the continent on an array of topics dealing with politics, economics, human rights and current affairs, Adetunji is frequently invited to speak on Africa's challenges and opportunities at conferences, such as the Brenthurst Foundation/ Konrad Adenauer Foundation, Africa's Swing States, Lake Como Italy 2015, corporate leadership sessions such as Dow Chemical, Expanding into Nigeria, Johnson and Johnson- Cape Town, Cliffe Dekker Hofmeyr Attorneys, 'Nigeria's challenges and the new government's response' and is a regular speaker at Gordon Institute of Business Sciences, the South Africa/ Nigeria Chamber of Commerce and the Institute of African Renaissance. Adetunji is a frequent speaker on the theme' Africa in the 21st century (The next 50 years). He is heavily connected to African Ambassadors, multi-lateral pan African organisations such as African Development Bank, NEPAD, UNECA, The African Union, Pan African Parliament and The Africa Progress Panel.

Books published: My Father and I (Memories of my father)

To learn more about Adetunji, visit www.adetunjiomotola.com; *Twitter @tunjiomotola*

16

ADAPTING EDUCATION
TO LEARNERS' NEEDS

Christian Nonso

The most populous nation in Africa, Nigeria is being touted by some analysts as an emerging major education market. The combination of a rapidly growing population and a burgeoning middle class has given rise to a substantial demand for quality education in Nigeria as well as significant opportunities for foreign education providers to meet growing needs.

With an estimated population of 200 million inhabitants and growing, Nigeria's population is expected to exceed that of the United States by 2050, and United Nations (UN) projections indicate that Nigeria could be the world's third most populous country by the end of the 21st century (UN Department of Economic and Social Affairs, 2019)

Although Africa has made progress in expanding school access in the past decade, it has the world's lowest secondary school enrolment rates. There currently are 15 million out-of-school children, including over 20% of children between the ages of about 6 and 11, a third between the ages of about 12 and 14, and nearly 60% between the ages of about 15 and 17 (UNESCO Institute of Statistics, 2021). The percentage of early tertiary age students are enrolled in higher education in sub-Saharan Africa is only 9.6%, which is significantly below the global average of 36% (UNESCO Institute of Statistics, 2018). To address this situation, a number of analysts have advocated for more schools and greater investment in education in Africa. The fourth Sustainable Development Goal highlights the importance of equitable access to a quality education as fundamental to improving individual's lives and enhancing development (UN Department of Economic and Social Affairs, 2015).

The United Nations (2021) reported that 'Major progress has been made towards increasing access to education at all levels and increasing enrolment rates in schools particularly for women and girls'. However, as they noted:

> Basic literacy skills have improved tremendously, yet bolder efforts are needed to make even greater strides for achieving universal education goals. For example, almost the entire world has achieved equality in primary education between girls and boys, but few countries have achieved that target at all levels of education while some countries are lagging behind in major key aspects of this development.

The World Economic Forum emphasised the importance of a quality education system for national and social development:

A strong education system broadens access to opportunities, improves health, and wellbeing and also boosts the resilience of communities, all while fuelling economic growth in a way that can reinforce and accelerate these processes. This type of education provides the skills people need to thrive in a new sustainable economy, working in areas such as renewable energy, smart agriculture, forest rehabilitation, the design of resource efficient cities, and sound management of healthy ecosystems. Perhaps most importantly, education can bring about a fundamental shift in how we think, act, and discharge our responsibilities toward one another and the planet. After all, while financial incentives, targeted policies, and technological innovation are needed to catalyse new ways of producing and consuming, they cannot reshape people's value systems so that they willingly uphold and advance the principles of sustainable development (Bokova & Figueres 2015).

However, schools in Africa 'can nurture a new generation of environmentally savvy citizens to support the transition to a prosperous and sustainable future' through the acquisition of quality education that is in compliance with the requirements of the information age (Bokova & Figueres 2015). True education is simply the process of developing the ability to learn, apply, unlearn, relearn, and engage in learning, training and practice so that one can develop expertise in a chosen career track. Some schools have become 'learning labs for sustainable development where young students are being prepared to adapt' to the requirements of the new information age in today's rapidly changing world (Bokova & Figueres 2015).

The ability to read and write are basic needs that must be acquired in order to achieve emancipation. An individual who possesses these two skills will have the power to enter into the future. The value of education is realised when people take ownership of those skills.

However, our society largely builds career success around certification, and it is unsurprising that so many graduates lack the basic learning skills to obtain a job or even determine a career path to which they can aspire. In our society, people lay more emphasis on schooling and obtaining a degree, regardless of whether or not the learner is suited to the career for which they are training.

In order to support youths' education, it is critical to provide them with a learning environment that can help them build their skills. We must support young people's skill acquisition and combine professional education with self-education (such as reading and writing) as they progress in their schooling. Once they are able to read and write, then youth will be able to unlock their own designed education, which should be a revolutionary education that is suited to their unique talents and abilities.

In order to help children, prepare for the jobs of the new future, it is critical that skill development be incorporated into school curricula. Children who are unable to read or write, perform simple mathematics, or implement verbal reasoning will struggle in a future in which a technological divide is rapidly emerging.

Soft skills are needed for the careers of the future, and anyone who wants to remain employed or obtain a high-flying job must devote their attention to acquiring and using them. In order to achieve this, it is important that students are taught creative thinking and analysis, problem-solving skills and cognitive thinking skills so that they can quickly adapt to a changing environment. Moreover, the coronavirus pandemic has posed further obstacles the changing world of learning, and it is essential that students rise up to meet this challenge. I appreciate that children and youth who live in rural areas within Africa may not necessarily have the opportunity to access online schooling or improve their prospects for relevant learning. Unfortunately, even before the pandemic, millions of children were not gaining these skillsets because they never started school, because they dropped out of school, or because their school does not offer a quality education.

According to data obtained from the United Nations Statistics Division (2021), 617 million children and adolescents world-wide are not proficient in either reading or mathematics. The implication of this situation is that a global learning crisis is looming, which will have devastating impacts on national poverty and inequality. Moreover, the recent coronavirus pandemic has also exerted a negative impact on children's and youths' opportunities to learn.

CONCLUSION

Collaborative efforts between private and public organisations are needed in order to improve educational outcomes and implement true education. The government must be able to invest in education and digital tools and ensure that it has the capability to withstand any pandemic that may arise in the future. Potential measures to enhance the education system in Nigeria include introducing courses such as coding and robotics and making them compulsory.

In order to achieve the above-described goals, investment in education should be made a priority, particularly for children living in rural areas and those from low-income families.

REFERENCES

Bokova, I. & Figueres, C. (2015, 19 May). Why education is the key to sustainable development. Retrieved from https://www.weforum.org/agenda/2015/05/why-education-is-the-key-to-sustainable-development/

United Nations (2021). *SDG4 - Quality education*. Retrieved from https://www.un.org/en/academic-impact/page/quality-education

United Nations Department of Economic and Social Affairs (2015). *Transforming our world: the 2030 Agenda for Sustainable Development*. Retrieved from https://www.un.org/ga/search/view_doc.asp?symbol=A/RES/70/1&Lang=E

United Nations Department of Economic and Social Affairs (2019). *World population prospects, 2019 revision.* Retrieved from https://population.un.org/wpp/

UNESCO Institute for Statistics (2018). *UIS 2018 data.* Retrieved from http://data.uis.unesco.org/

UNESCO Institute for Statistics (2021). *Education in Africa.* Retrieved from http://uis.unesco.org/en/topic/education-africa

United Nations Statistics Division (2021). *Shockingly low proficiency rates in reading and mathematics signal a global learning crisis.* Retrieved from https://unstats.un.org/sdgs/report/2019/goal-04/

BIOGRAPHY

Christian Nonso

Christian Nonso is a Revolutionary Mastery of Education and Business', who combines the mastery of new revolutionary education with the trend of the 21st century business enterprise development and deployment, with the capacity to give even a school dropout leverage to succeed in our new economic realities. With his new revolutionary education, he has birthed witty inventions through people without respect to formal education qualifications. He is the founder and principal consultant at LegacyXpact™ Consulting Limited. Christian is a graduate and alumni of several business schools like Fate Foundation Business School Lagos, Creative Entrepreneurs South Africa etc.

He is a Mental Reformer, an Author, a futurist [in education], best Retail and Small Business Strategist and a preacher of God's word. Christian has delivered speeches, lectures, trainings, coaching and mental revival™ in various places across churches, conferences, seminars, virtual trainings, boardrooms, schools [at all levels, with over 50 tuition centres and schools. Christian is a graduate and alumni of several business schools like Fate Foundation Business School Lagos, Creative Entrepreneurs South Africa etc. He is one of those strongly championing the new course of MENTAL REVIVAL™ AND REVOLUTION in youths/students, school dropouts, graduates and educational sector in Nigeria through the revealing of the encoded and coded secrets of the conspiracies of education by the introduction of a new type of education known as MENTAL REVIVAL™ FORM OF EDUCATION.

He has written five revolutionary books titled: - My Breakthrough Experience: Revolutionary Approach to Personal Change in Crises. - The Conspiracy Of Education Decoded: The New Definition Of Mental Revolution and Educational System Reformation. - NYSC Is A Conspiracy: Breaking The Laws Of Conformity. - Breaking the Strongholds of Schooling: A New World of Possibilities. - Manual for Personal Education Revolution: Leveraging On the New Realities of Education for Personal & Corporate Productivity

Phone Numbers: Call: +2348067482341, WhatsApp Enabled: +2348146264874. Email: legacyxpat@gmail.com Twitter handle: @Legacyxpat

Printed in Great Britain
by Amazon

23771358R00145